The 500 Hidden Secrets of

STOCKHOLM

INTRODUCTION

This book aims to help you discover the best of Stockholm behind its idyllic, water-surrounded façade. On the one hand, Stockholm is a dynamic capital where influences from all over the world merge and have an impact on restaurants, hotels, and cultural institutions. A city that has put itself on the map as a hub of innovation and creativity. If you're looking for avant-garde restaurants, art museums in the suburbs, or natural wine bars, you'll find them here. On the other hand, Stockholm's Nordic heritage is tangible in everything, from historical buildings over traditional *fika* to minimalistic design. Effervescent modernity and timeless, undeniable beauty: Stockholm offers the best of both worlds.

The inner-city centre is manageable in terms of size in addition to being pedestrian-friendly. You'll also understand better how the islands and neighbourhoods are linked if you explore this part of the city on foot. The metro system – also the world's longest art exhibition – takes you to the different districts outside the well-visited city centre. Veer off the beaten path and you won't be disappointed as Stockholm is a vibrant capital with much to offer.

In this book, overrated tourist traps have been left out in favour of tucked-away discoveries that will surprise foreign Swedophiles and knowledgeable locals. Uncover charming peculiarities and intriguing titbits about renowned landmarks or find new favourites. This guide is your ticket to a host of secret gems where you can experience the authentic atmosphere of Stockholm for yourself.

HOW TO
USE THIS BOOK?

This guide lists 500 things you need to know about Stockholm in 100 different categories. Most of these are places to visit, with practical information to help you find your way. Others are bits of information that help you get to know the city and its habitants. The aim of this guide is to inspire, not to cover the city from A to Z.

The places listed in the guide are given an address, including the neighbourhood, and a number. The neighbourhood and number allow you to find the locations on the maps at the beginning of the book: first look for the map of the corresponding neighbourhood, then look for the right number. A word of caution: these maps are not detailed enough to allow you to find specific locations in the city. You can obtain an excellent map from any tourist office or in most hotels. Or the addresses can be located on a smartphone.

Please also bear in mind that cities change all the time. The chef who hits a high note one day may be uninspiring on the day you happen to visit. The hotel ecstatically reviewed in this book might suddenly go downhill under a new manager. The bar considered one of the 5 not-to-miss cocktail bars might be empty on the night you visit. This is obviously a highly personal selection. You might not always agree with it. If you want to leave a comment, recommend a bar or reveal your favourite secret place, please visit the website *the500hiddensecrets.com* – you'll also find free tips and the latest news about the series there – or follow *@500hiddensecrets* on Instagram or Facebook and leave a comment.

THE AUTHOR

Antonia af Petersens grew up in Stockholm and works as a freelance writer and journalist. She has contributed to various Swedish newspapers, web publications, and lifestyle magazines. She is also the author of the interior book *New Nordic Colour* (UK).

Antonia's lifelong Stockholm journey has taken her through diverse neighbourhoods. She has called many places home, from the historic heart of Gamla stan, where she was born, to cosy Birkastan and water-embedded Kungsholmen. She now lives in Östermalm, where she and her family enjoy easy access to museums, cultural events, and green spaces. While she knows every street and alley, her insatiable curiosity drives her to seek new experiences and perspectives. Driven by a constant desire to uncover hidden gems, Antonia embraces Stockholm's endless possibilities.

The author wishes to thank her friends who generously shared their favourites in Stockholm. Thanks to everyone at Luster, in particular to Dettie Luyten and Katya Doms, for their kind guidance while writing this book. Nadja Endler, thanks for travelling all over Stockholm to capture the city's versatility. Lastly, the author's family deserves immense recognition for their patience and encouragement. Thanks to Axel, August, and Bill for joining on bike rides, exploring new playgrounds, and accommodating detours. Thanks also to Mum, Peter, and Grandma Iris for babysitting duty during restaurant visits. All this unwavering support has been instrumental to the writing of this book and has made the research and writing journey a joyous adventure. Antonia hopes this work will help readers to establish their own unique relationship with her hometown.

STOCKHOLM

overview

Hagaparken

9
Solna
Stockholm North

7
Vasastan

8
Kungsholmen

1
Norrmalm

2
Östermalm

3
Gamla stan

6
Skepps-
holmen

6
Djurgården

Riddarfjärden

4
Midsommarkransen
Aspudden
Liljeholmen
Lilla Essingen

5
Södermalm

Map 1
NORRMALM

Map 2
ÖSTERMALM

Map 3
GAMLA STAN

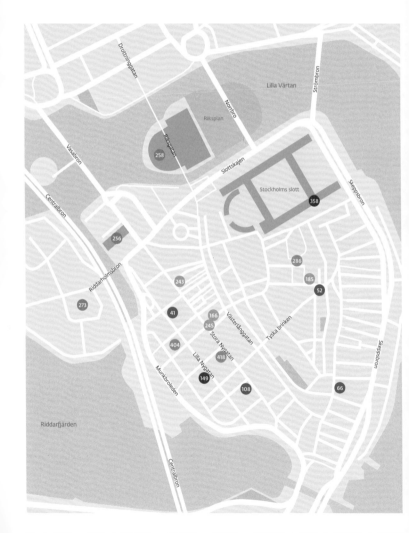

Map 4
MIDSOMMARKRANSEN, ASPUDDEN, LILJEHOLMEN
and SÖDERMALM

Map 5
SÖDERMALM

Map 6

SKEPPSHOLMEN
and DJURGÅRDEN

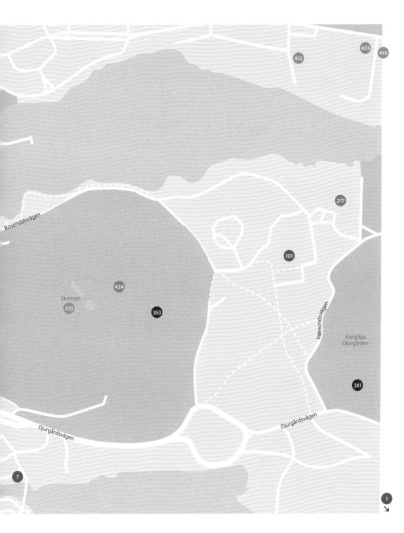

Rosendalsvägen

412

405 410

277

101

Valmundsvägen

424

Skansen

310

363

Kungliga
Djurgården

381

Djurgårdsvägen

Djurgårdsvägen

7

1
↘

Map 7
VASASTAN

Map 8
KUNGSHOLMEN

EAT — **DRINK** — SHOP — BUILDINGS — DISCOVER — **CULTURE** — CHILDREN — SLEEP — WEEKEND — RANDOM

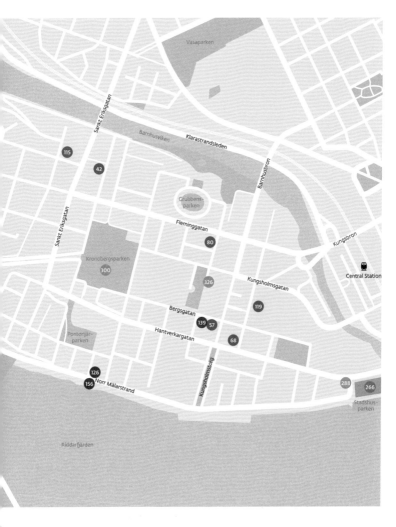

Map 9
SOLNA *and*
STOCKHOLM NORTH

Tranholmen

Lilla Värtan

Stockholm
University

421

Laduviken

Norra Djurgården

456

468 401

Lidingövägen

Norra Länken

Valhallavägen

299

ADAM/ALBIN

120 PLACES TO EAT OR BUY GOOD FOOD

---

5 of the best restaurants for
NEW NORDIC CUISINE

---

1 **AIRA**
   Biskopsvägen 9
   Djurgården ⑥
   +46 (0)8 480 049 00
   aira.se

Michelin-starred Aira is situated at the far end of Biskopsudden in Djurgården. Try the splendid star-quality tasting menu. Tip: Don't miss Skippers Inn, their pop-up on the terrace which is open during the summer months and has a more relaxed ambience.

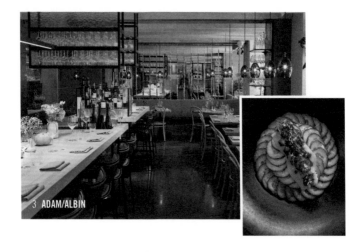

3 ADAM/ALBIN

2 NOUR

AT: TOWNHOUSE NOSH
AND CHOW
Norrlandsgatan 24
Norrmalm ①
+46 (0)8 503 389 71
restaurantnour.se

Anyone who has already eaten at any of Chef Sayan Isaksson's award-winning restaurants will recognise his signature subtle fusion of Scandinavian and Japanese cuisine. Although the prices are high, each small dish has been lovingly prepared, and is beautifully presented like a small work of art.

3 ADAM/ALBIN

Rådmansgatan 16
Vasastan ⑦
+46 (0)8 411 55 35
adamalbin.se

ADAM/ALBIN has a local and international feel at the same time. The duo is inspired by food from all over the world, creating a casual fine dining experience with Nordic roots. They serve a five-course tasting menu but you can have a seat at the bar and take your pick from the menu.

4 FRANTZÉN

Klara Norra
kyrkogata 26
Norrmalm ①
+46 (0)8 20 85 80
restaurantfrantzen.com

Frantzén is one of the world's best restaurants. The concept is completely in tune with the new style of Nordic cuisine, where sustainability and nature and its seasons determine what you will find on your plate. While the price may seem intimidating, the atmosphere is inviting and the service exceptional.

5 EKSTEDT

Humlegårdsgatan 17
Östermalm ②
+46 (0)8 611 12 10
ekstedt.nu

Traditional cuisine, including cooking over open fire, is all the rage again. Plenty of praise has been heaped on Ekstedt over the years. Many of the cooking techniques they use here date back to the days before electricity was invented. No electric cookers here, just heat, smoke, soot, ash and fire.

The 5 cosiest places to
EAT BY THE WATER

---

6 TORPEDVERKSTAN
Norra Brobänken
Skeppsholmen ⑥
+46 (0)8 611 41 00
torpedverkstan.se

Torpedverkstan is located in a workshop from the 1890s on the idyllic island of Skeppsholmen. This is a great spot to enjoy that archipelago vibe in the heart of the city with charming views of the old ships along the dock.

7 SLIPEN
Beckholmsvägen 26
Djurgården ⑥
+46 (0)8 551 531 05
slipen.se

The couple behind the Fabrique bakeries have stepped up their game, moving from bread and buns to open Slipen. This place can be a bit difficult to find but once there, you will love the bistro, wine bar, bakery and cafe with lovely views of Beckholmen Island through the large windows.

8 LUX DAG FÖR DAG
Primusgatan 116
Lilla Essingen ④
+46 (0)8 619 01 90
luxdagfordag.se

You'll find some of the city's freshest food in this beautiful early-20th-century brick building along the seafront of Lilla Essingen. LUX Dag för Dag works with many local, small producers who supply this restaurant with the best seasonal products or the catch of the day.

9 SKROTEN

Beckholmsvägen 14
Djurgården ⑥
+46 (0)70 380 80 80
skrotens.se

Skroten is one of Stockholm's well-kept secrets, tucked away among the docks and shipyards in Djurgården. Enjoy a bowl of their perfectly cooked fish stew with a glass of wine or a coffee with a slice of raspberry pie while you take in the ship's lanterns, creaky floorboards, life buoys and the pleasant scent of tar.

10 SPRITMUSEUM

Djurgårdsstrand 9
Djurgården ⑥
+46 (0)8 121 313 09
spritmuseum.se

Spritmuseum and its restaurant are housed in one of the Swedish navy's last remaining galley sheds from the 18th century. From here you can see Skeppsholmen and catch a glimpse of the heights of Söder but first of all this place is worth a visit for its innovative Nordic cuisine and fantastic service.

7 SLIPEN

The 5 best places for
FISH AND SEAFOOD

---

11 STUREHOF

Stureplan 2
Östermalm ①
+46 (0)8 440 57 30
sturehof.com

Guests love the top-class seafood and great ambience at this centuries-old brasserie. The rest of Stockholm may be sound asleep, but you will always receive a warm welcome at Sturehof because of its generous opening hours, seven days a week.

12 B.A.R.

Blasieholmsgatan 4-A
Norrmalm ②
+46 (0)8 611 53 35
restaurangbar.se

B.A.R. is an interesting mix of a restaurant and a marketplace. Located along elegant Blasieholmen, this place is a meeting point for fish-lovers, who either eat on site or stop for a takeaway on their way home from work. The dining area is surrounded by aquariums, scales and ice-filled counters, displaying the catch of the day.

13 LE BISTROT DE WASAHOF

Dalagatan 46
Vasastan ⑦
+46 (0)8 32 34 40
wasahof.se

If you love a French take on fish and shellfish, then Wasahof, opposite Vasaparken, is the place for you. Enjoy all the best the sea has to offer, to the tune of classical music and opera. Don't forget to taste Wasahof's speciality, oysters. The oyster bar serves a cornucopia of tasty varieties from different countries.

14 WEDHOLMS FISK

Arsenalsgatan 1
Norrmalm ②
+46 (0)8 611 78 74
wedholmsfisk.se

White table-cloths, a fancy address, impeccable service and traditional cuisine. Does this sound right up your alley? Wedholms Fisk has hosted royals and celebrities over the years. The menu features a range of classic dishes, making it a great option for anyone who is not a slave to trends and enjoys a nice culinary experience.

15 DEN GAMLE OCH HAVET

Tulegatan 27
Vasastan ⑦
+46 (0)8 661 53 00
dengamleochhavet.se

Italian cuisine has a knack for creating magic out of seemingly simple ingredients and Den Gamle och Havet does just that. The Campogiani family serves dishes such as fish fillets in butter sauce, Risotto alla Marinara or delicious deep-fried seafood. You will not be disappointed at this Italian gem in Vasastan.

11 STUREHOF

5 places to enjoy
SEASONAL DINING

---

16 **VÄXTHUSET**
Hammarby
Slussväg 2
Södermalm ⑤
+46 (0)8 644 20 33
restaurangvaxthuset.se

Växthuset, located under Skanstullsbron bridge, caters to vegetarians as well as to people who are interested in a flexitarian lifestyle, but have yet to see the benefits of eating vegetarian. Guests are encouraged to order several dishes to share at this restaurant, which pairs seasonal ingredients with international flavours.

17 **EMMER**
AT: ULRIKSDALS VÄRDSHUS
Ulriksdals Slottspark
Solna ⑨
+46 (0)8 85 08 15
restaurangemmer.se

Emmer is located in the beautiful Ulriksdals Värdshus and is open during the warmer months of the year and in December for Christmas. The restaurant's seasonal menu features modern, Scandinavian food with vegetables which they grow themselves in the garden outside. It doesn't get more local than this.

18 BRUTALISTEN

Regeringsgatan 71
Norrmalm ①
+46 (0)72 161 86 83
brutalisten.com

The experimental menu at Brutalisten is updated daily and divided into three categories: 'orthodox-brutalist' with a single ingredient, 'brutalist' or the single ingredient plus salt and water, and 'semi-brutalist' where dishes may contain several ingredients. By varying the time, temperature and cooking method, edible magic is created.

19 RUTABAGA

AT: GRAND HÔTEL
Södra Blasieholms-
hamnen 6
Norrmalm ②
+46 (0)8 679 35 84
mdghs.se/rutabaga

This is Stockholm's first high-end strictly vegetarian restaurant. At Rutabaga (old Swedish for turnip), the famous chef Mathias Dahlgren proves that high-quality greens and roots can be transformed into outstanding dishes. He is mainly inspired by international cuisine but all his dishes have that quintessential simple, yet innovative, Scandi twist.

20 PETRI

Kommendörs-
gatan 16
Östermalm ②
+46 (0)70 741 17 42
petrirestaurant.com

Petter Nillson's Petri is located behind arched windows in Östermalm's fancier neighbourhood. The ambitious, nature-oriented tasting menu features ten courses, using in-season ingredients to present unique dishes. The minimalistic, elegant interior acts as a sleek backdrop for their amazing, often vegetable-based dishes.

The 5 best places for
KÖTTBULLAR
(meatballs)

---

21 OPERAKÄLLAREN BAKFICKAN
AT: OPERAHUSET
Karl XII:s torg
Norrmalm ①
+46 (0)8 676 58 09
operakallaren.se

No visit to Stockholm would be quite complete without a taste of Swedish meatballs. At Bakfickan, the Operakällaren's more casual venue, you can enjoy this Swedish dish just like traditionalists believe it should be eaten – served with mashed potatoes, a cream sauce, lingonberries and pickled cucumbers. A dish that will please guests of all ages.

22 TRANAN

22 TRANAN

Karlbergsvägen 14
Vasastan ⑦
+46 (0)8 676 58 09
tranan.se

At Tranan, it's all about the meatballs. Even when they're not on the menu, people still order them. So follow suit and as you bite into these golden-brown little beauties you will immediately understand why they are the star of the menu, which, to be fair, features plenty of other delicious dishes, too.

23 RICHE

Birger Jarlsgatan 4
Östermalm ②
+46 (0)8 545 035 60
riche.se

Tore Wretman was the man who put French brasserie food and traditional Swedish dishes on the menu at Riche. This quirky, French-style, 19th-century house has been a popular fixture for many years. If you are to pick only one restaurant for a great experience, Riche is your best bet.

24 MEATBALLS FOR THE PEOPLE

Nytorgsgatan 30
Södermalm ⑤
+46 (0)8 466 60 99
meatball.se

The team behind this place has taken the liberty to create their take on Sweden's beloved meatballs. Here they serve organic meatballs in a variety of flavours, from classic meaty ones to more innovative versions with ingredients like salmon or vegetables. You can either eat on-site or buy meatballs to take away.

25 PRINSEN

Mäster Samuelsgatan 4
Norrmalm ②
+46 (0)8 684 238 11
restaurangprinsen.se

Mythical Prinsen has served classic cuisine to Stockholmers, artists, writers, workers, directors and visitors since 1897. They have retained the place's unique character and decor. Let the cloakroom attendant take your jacket, sit down at one of the tables and order their famous meatballs.

5 spots for a
NOURISHING LUNCH

26 **KALF & HANSEN**
Mariatorget 2
Södermalm ⑤
+46 (0)8 551 531 51
kalfochhansen.se

Rune Kalf Hansen and his son Fabian run their casual fast food restaurant in Mariatorget together. They have received several awards and many regulars have already returned to sample their Nordic organic fast food of meat, fish or vegetarian meatballs with healthy side dishes. All the meatballs are completely lactose and gluten-free.

27 **À LA LO**
Birger Jarlsgatan 77
Vasastan ⑦
+46 (0)70 713 87 87
alalo.se

This hip, French-inspired gem, which attracts a young crowd, is run by a mother and daughter. Everything is plant-based here, down to the famous croissants. À la Lo serves classic French fare such as *pain perdu* as well as fresh salads and basil&matcha lemonade.

28 **MAHALO**
Odengatan 26
Vasastan ⑦
+46 (0)73 729 54 53
mahalosthlm.se

The first thing you see, when entering Mahalo's Vasastan venue, is a neon sign saying 'Vegan is the new black' – here everything they serve is plant-based. Take a brief break from busy Odengatan and try the fruity 'Pussy Power' or sample some of their fresh rainbow salads.

29 DR. MAT

Tegnérgatan 5
Vasastan ⑦
+46 (0)70 615 32 22
doktormat.se

Dr. Mat takes dietetics seriously. The ingredients in each dish are selected and combined for the greatest possible health benefits. Dr. Mat's self-fermented vegetables are full of good bacteria that benefit the gut and strengthen our immune system. Dr. Mat proves that nutritious food can also be yummy.

30 KALE & CRAVE

Roslagsgatan 2
Vasastan ⑦
+46 (0)70 978 65 98
kaleandcrave.se

Kale & Crave was founded by a bunch of Swedish superstar DJs who wanted to bring the healthy aspects of California's food culture to Stockholm. This place has become quite the meeting point for food-conscious musicians, bloggers and athletes. What do they have to offer apart from a cool crowd? Food that has been prepared without sugar, lactose and gluten. Oh, and kale obviously.

33 K-MÄRKT

The 5 best places for a
LONG LUNCH

---

31 URBAN DELI NYTORGET

Nytorget 4
Södermalm ⑤
+46 (0)8 425 500 30
urbandeli.org/nytorget

A grocery store, bar and restaurant under the same roof – Urban Deli's concept at Nytorget in SoFo is always busy. Locals, actors and other personalities, friends and food aficionados from all over the city gather in what has almost become Söder's common living room and kitchen.

32 DOMA

Nybrogatan 48
Östermalm ②
+46 (0)8 684 292 82
doma.se

Cook and pastry chef Dorothea Malmegård and her husband run DoMa on Nybrogatan. There are very few places that succeed in combining such a laidback atmosphere with great personal style. The restaurant is literally an extension of their living room as they live in the same building and used to host brunch-supper clubs in their flat before deciding to open a restaurant.

33 K-MÄRKT

Karlavägen 100
Östermalm ②
+46 (0)8 466 88 90
kmarkt.se

K-märkt is located in a seventies office building. The house itself is an important architectural feature in the cityscape of Stockholm – but K-märkt is definitely worth a visit for other reasons as well. In an effort to reduce food waste the lunch buffet guests pay for their food by weight.

34 BOBERGS MATSAL

AT: NK DEPARTMENT STORE
Hamngatan 18-20
Norrmalm ①
+46 (0)8 762 81 61
bobergsmatsal.se

Like any self-respecting fancy department store in a major city, Stockholm's NK also has an upscale restaurant. Head to the top floor to find Bobergs Matsal, the perfect stop for a luxurious three meal-lunch, lovingly prepared for you by Michelin starred-chef Björn Frantzén and his team.

35 RESTAURANG HANTVERKET

Sturegatan 15
Östermalm ②
+46 (0)8 121 321 60
restauranghantverket.se

In this restaurant close to Humlegården, you can get a taste of the traditional Swedish legacy but in a new style. *Hantverket* means craftsmanship and that philosophy permeates the lunch menu. Visit Hantverket if you want to try a modern take on traditional Swedish flavours.

The 5 best
ASIAN restaurants

---

36 SUSHI SHO

Upplandsgatan 45
Vasastan ⑦
+46 (0)8 30 30 30
sushisho.se

Interested in trying Scandi-style Edomae sushi? Head to Sushi Sho in Vasastan. But do book beforehand since this small place only has twelve seats at the bar and four on a sofa. All guests are served each course from the fixed price menu at the same time, by the chef.

37 FARANG

Tulegatan 7
Vasastan ⑦
+46 (0)8 673 74 00
farang.se

Farang stands out from the other restaurants of its kind because it is the opposite of a hidden place. The huge, dark premises and industrial interior refer to the site's former use, as a power station. The shared food concept puts Southeast Asian cuisine in the spotlight.

38 TENGU

Rådmansgatan 12
Östermalm ②
+46 (0)8 30 39 89
tengu.se

Tengu is housed in the architecture school's old premises, a 1960s brutalist, concrete building. The restaurant serves slurp-worthy ramen cooked in a savoury broth but even though the food is delicious, guests also value Tengu's trendy setting, hugely likable staff and lively vibe.

39 MISSHUMASSHU

AT: BIRGER JARLSPASSAGE
Smålandsgatan 10
Norrmalm ②
+46 (0)8 425 125 50
misshumasshu.se

Skewers, bowls, steamed vegetables, ramen, ... The range at Misshumasshu spans a broad Asian spectrum with an added emphasis on Japanese cuisine. This vibrant diner/liquor bar mash up contrasts beautifully with the elegant 19th-century passage where it is located. The magnificent gallery is worth a visit in itself.

40 INDIO

Kocksgatan 52
Södermalm ⑤
+46 (0)8 420 620 20
indio.se/kitchen-kocksgatan

What do Japanese and Peruvian food have in common? A penchant for raw fish. At Indio they have created a fusion of both. Enjoy *sashimi*, *ceviche* and *edamame* surrounded by pale wood surfaces and raw concrete walls at Sweden's first Nikkei restaurant in the very heart of Södermalm's most hipsteresque neighbourhood.

39 MISSHUMASSHU

5 places for
NOSE TO TAIL-EATING

---

41 BAKFICKAN DJURET
Lilla Nygatan 5
Gamla stan ③
+46 (0)8 506 400 84
djuret.se

Djuret means 'animal' in Swedish, so you can see how meat lovers will not be disappointed here. The constantly updated menu features seasonal ingredients from the land and the sea. At Djuret each ingredient is cooked in a way that maximises your gastronomic experience.

42 AG
Kronobergsgatan 37
Kungsholmen ⑧
+46 (0)8 410 681 00
restaurangag.se

Restaurant AG is hidden away in an anonymous house in Kungsholmen. This place used to be a silversmith's workshop. AG (the chemical symbol for silver) is famous for its meat dishes and you can see quarters of meat hanging in a row in the large fridge at the entrance.

43 LENNART & BROR
Birger Jarlsgatan 83
Vasastan ⑦
+46 (0)8 612 45 15
lennartochbror.se

Lennart & Bror is a tiny, fully tiled deli that also serves simple lunches and dinners a few times a week. Every piece of meat is hand-picked by the owners Fritjof and Rasmus at the slaughterhouse. Tip: the style of their fish restaurant in Tegnérgatan is very similar.

44 SVARTENGRENS

Tulegatan 24
Vasastan ⑦
+46 (0)8 612 65 50
svartengrens.se

Svartengrens only uses locally raised beef from the Stockholm archipelago. They also believe in doing everything from scratch, from smoking their own bacon to cooking their stock with bones from the same farms where they source their meat. If the restaurant is fully booked, then check out the bar.

45 ROLFS KÖK

Tegnérgatan 41
Vasastan ⑦
+46 (0)8 10 16 96
rolfskok.se

With its tasty food and iconic interior by designers Jonas Bohlin and Thomas Sandell, Rolf's kitchen has been a modern classic on Stockholm's restaurant scene since 1989. Grilled bone marrow, pork confit, ox cheek braised in red wine – the chefs know exactly how to create magic with unusual ingredients.

The 5 tastiest
FAST-FOOD
places

---

46 FALAFELBAREN

Götgatan 96
Södermalm ⑤
+46 (0)72 907 726 37
falafelbaren.se

If you suddenly have a craving for falafel with pickles and tahini sauce while visiting Stockholm, go to Falafelbaren, near Skanstull. All their dishes are vegetarian and in addition to falafel, they also serve homemade *börek*, *shackshuka* and *fool*. They have a couple of bar tables if you want to eat on-site.

47 HASSELSSON

Sankt Eriksgatan 67
Vasastan ⑦
+46 (0)70 339 30 91
hasselsson.com

Hasselsson's reinterpretations of fast food from the sea, like fish and chips and moules frites, have proven quite popular. Wet your whistle with a pint of their Li'l Pils, their take on pilsner which they brew themselves. Try to get a table (there are just a few!) or eat your freshly fried meal on the hoof.

48 SCANDWICH

Malmskillnads-
gatan 17
Norrmalm ①
+46 (0)73 344 11 90
scandwich.se

Many locals have become addicted to Scandwich's delicious sandwiches – to the extent that lunch guests now bump into the same familiar faces (several times during the same week)... All their artisanal sandwiches are made from scratch and the brothers who own the joint were even crowned the winners of the Swedish Sandwich Championships one year.

49 LA NETA

Barnhusgatan 2
Norrmalm ①
+46 (0)8 411 58 80
laneta.se

Did you know that the Swedes and the Norwegians eat the most tacos in Europe? *Taquería* La Neta is the perfect place for taco lovers. Here hard shells, chopped cucumber and canned maize have been replaced with authentic ingredients such as *bistec*, *campechana* and *rajas con queso*.

50 BAROBAO

Hornsgatan 66
Södermalm ⑤
+46 (0)8 643 77 76
barobao.com

You'll find this Japanese-Taiwanese restaurant in bustling and busy Hornsgatan. Here they serve amazing baos with a Nordic twist. These white, fluffy and steamed buns with interesting fillings could be described as an Asian, tasty equivalent to burgers. Barobao offers flavourful dishes at great prices in a relaxed, minimalistic setting.

5 of the most
ROMANTIC
places to eat

---

51 PERSONA

Torstenssonsgatan 11
Östermalm ②
personasthlm.com

Can you think of anything more romantic than feeling truly unique? At Persona, they go out of their way to make all their diners feel seen and special, with their customised fine dining concept. Everything starts with a conversation about what you feel like drinking and which meal would pair nicely with your drink. Also a great opportunity to get an insight into what tantalises your date's tastebuds.

52 PASTIS

Baggensgatan 12
Gamla stan ⑤
+46 (0)8 20 20 18
pastis.se

This teeny-tiny place, which serves French cuisine, is tucked away in one of the cosy alleys of the Old Town. It can get pretty cramped, as they can only seat about 20. Then again, the tiny tables are packed closely together, forcing you to lean in more closely for intimate conversations and undeniably contributing to the amorous vibe.

53 CHEZ JOLIE

Ingmar Bergmans gata 2
Östermalm ②
+46 (0)8 527 757 90
chezjolie.se

Chez Jolie embraces Frenchitude in the most glamorous way. The elegant setting with velvet sofas in blush tones, solid oak furniture, marble, and decorative mirrors provides a luxurious framework for the rustic food they serve. Just the perfect venue to celebrate a special occasions, en tête-à-tête or with a larger group.

54 CAFÉ NIZZA

Åsögatan 171
Södermalm ⑤
+46 (0)8 640 99 50
cafenizza.se

The atmosphere at Café Nizza is perfect for a romantic but easy-going date. This cosy place with its checkerboard tiled floors, white table-cloths, Thonet chairs and terrazzo tables has an inviting bar and affordable prices. Expect to be surrounded by locals enjoying the nice food on the menu (that is frequently updated) or a glass of good wine.

55 HOMMAGE

Krukmakargatan 22
Södermalm ⑤
+46 (0)8 658 42 50
hommage.se

Lovebirds who pine for Paris should visit Hommage, close to Mariatorget. Behind the arched doors of a former fire station, a lovely French restaurant with bentwood chairs and a warm atmosphere awaits. On summer evenings tables spill out onto the street so only a narrow pavement separates passers-by from the bistro buzz.

55 HOMMAGE

5

FREELANCER FAVOURITES

---

56 **KAFFEVERKET**
Sankt Eriksgatan 88
Vasastan ⑦
+46 (0)8 31 51 42
kaffeverket.se

Working in a cafe is becoming increasingly normal in Stockholm. Kaffeverket, next to Sankt Eriksplan, is a hot spot for many freelancers. Eavesdrop on the people next to you as they are holding casual meetings, watch students work hard or have a peak at one of the many laptop screens while you're enjoying breakfast, lunch or *fika*.

57 **IL CAFFÈ**
Bergsgatan 17
Kungsholmen ⑧
+46 (0)8 652 30 04
ilcaffe.se

Il Caffè is often referred to as one of Stockholm's first freelancer cafes. Since 1996, this cafe is the place to go for great coffee, tasty pastries, friendly conversations, an unpretentious atmosphere and an inner courtyard. Nowadays you can find Il Caffè all over Stockholm (and even Los Angeles) but it all started at Kungsholmen.

58 KAFFEBAR

Bysistorget 6
Södermalm ⑤
+46 (0)76 875 29 92

Kaffebar at Bysistorget is the unofficial go-to for locals in the neighbourhood looking for a place to work. They serve really good coffee, sandwiches, and freshly squeezed juices. They also have internet and several tables with power outlets. Try to go in April/May when the cherry trees outside the window are in full bloom.

59 GAST

Rådmansgatan 57
Vasastan ⑦
+46 (0)8 27 02 22
gastcafe.se

One of Stockholm's best-looking cafes is Gast. Here iconic Scandinavian chairs in pale wood are combined with a warm palette of pink, apricot and nude. Gast serves healthy salads, juices and hot beverages. The location is great, between the City and Vasastan in front of Observatorielunden.

60 CAFÉ PASCAL

Norrtullsgatan 4
Vasastan ⑦
+46 (0)8 31 61 10
cafepascal.se

Coffee and sandwich lovers have discovered their own little cafe heaven just one block from busy Odenplan. Café Pascal is run by three siblings and everything here is locally produced, from the coffee to the delicious pastries. The coffee is sourced from carefully selected roasteries and the sandwiches are in a league of their own.

The 5 best places for a
FABULOUS BREAKFAST

---

61 **BANACADO**
   Tegnérgatan 6
   Norrmalm ①
   +46 (0)8 474 86 04
   banacado.com

As you may have guessed, Banacado is a combination of banana and avocado, two of the main ingredients on the menu of this 'all-day breakfast' joint. The menu is 100% plant-based and free from gluten and refined sugar. The pale-yellow decorative scheme matches the pastel smoothie bowls. It's as if the sun is always shining here, even on a cloudy day.

62 **KONSTHALLEN**
   Allmänna gränd 2
   Djurgården ⑥
   +46 (0)72 080 82 49
   konsthallen.com

Take the morning boat from Slussen to Djurgården (only seven minutes) for an opportunity to enjoy everything you might want for breakfast. Take your pick, for a fixed price, from a buffet laden with freshly baked bread and croissants from Konsthallen's bakery next door, as well as spreads, cheese, oatmeal porridge, overnight oats… The options are endless!

63 POM & FLORA

Bondegatan 64
Södermalm ⑤
+46 (0)76 030 32 80
pomochflora.se

Pom & Flora has a modern menu and innovative breakfast options with ingredients that even the knowledgeable foodie might have to google. Their avocado toast and colourful bowls are probably among Stockholm's most photogenic breakfasts. And everything tastes just as good as it looks.

64 GREASY SPOON

Hagagatan 4
Vasastan ⑦
greasyspoon.se

Greasy Spoon is the place to go for brekkie and brunch all day long. Their Anglo-Saxon menu includes classics like buckwheat pancakes and eggs Benedict with a modern twist. They do not take bookings, so you are welcome to drop in and grab a table or add your name to the waiting list.

65 BROMS

Karlavägen 76
Östermalm ②
+46 (0)8 26 37 10
bromskarlaplan.se

Despite its upscale address, the ambience at Broms tends to be rather laidback. This bistro is open from early morning and feels like a living room. They serve breakfast on weekdays and brunch on Saturdays and Sundays. Raise a toast to the weekend with a classic cocktail, to go with their savoury, crispy brunch dishes.

5

MYTHICAL RESTAURANTS

---

66 **DEN GYLDENE FREDEN**
Österlånggatan 51
Gamla stan ③
+46 (0)8 24 97 60
gyldenefreden.se

This unique tavern from 1722 has welcomed many nationally famous poets, writers and songwriters. In the early 1900s, artist Anders Zorn bought the house to save the restaurant from shutting down. He later left it to The Swedish Academy, which still convenes here every Thursday for its weekly dinner.

67 **TENNSTOPET**
Dalagatan 50
Vasastan ⑦
+46 (0)8 32 25 18
tennstopet.se

If you visit only one mythical restaurant while in Stockholm, then choose Tennstopet. This place provides a glimpse of Stockholm in the old days. It owes its reputation to its audience of journalists and writers but also to the fermented Baltic herring they serve in August each year.

68 **MÄSTER ANDERS**
Pipersgatan 1
Kungsholmen ⑧
+46 (0)8 654 20 01
masteranders.se

The bistro interior is patinated with age, in a chic and authentic way. The globe pendant lights, yellow tiles and the hexagon-patterned floor have become trendy several times over. Here you can eat classics and peek discreetly at the famous media personalities at the table next to you.

69 PELIKAN

Blekingegatan 40
Södermalm ⑤
+46 (0)8 556 090 90
pelikan.se

Pelikan is for anyone who wants to experience the 'authentic' Södermalm. This beer cafe, which is over 300 years old, has been located at its current address since 1904 and has attracted many artists. People usually start in Pelikan and then move on to the equally mythical and famous pub Kvarnen, six blocks away. The locals call this 'doing a Pelikvarn'.

70 KONSTNÄRSBAREN

Smålandsgatan 7
Norrmalm ②
+46 (0)8 679 60 32
konstnarsbaren.se

In the 1930s, Konstnärsbaren was the place to go to for artists. The interior is still largely intact with unique murals painted by such artists as Isaac Grünewald and Einar Forseth, but nowadays they've added contemporary art. This place has never ceased to be a meeting point in the heart of Stockholm.

66 DEN GYLDENE FREDEN

5 restaurants with
A GREAT VIEW

---

71 **FOTOGRAFISKA**
Stadsgårds-
hamnen 22
Södermalm ⑤
+46 (0)8 509 005 30
fotografiska.com

Stockholm's museum of photography and its great restaurant offer lovely views of the capital's inlet. The menu here is all about sustainability and vegetables and guests will soon realise what is the season by observing nature's colours as they change outside the windows, and by enjoying the excellent fare on their plate.

71 FOTOGRAFISKA

72 HIMLEN
AT: SKRAPAN
Götgatan 78
Södermalm ⑤
+46 (0)8 660 60 68
restauranghimlen.se

On the 26th floor of 'Skrapan' you will find one of Stockholm's best views and great French and Swedish cuisine. This sixties building is a well-known landmark in the capital's southern district and used to be the headquarters of the Swedish tax office and, at one time, Europe's tallest building.

73 ARC
AT: BLIQUE BY NOBIS
Gävlegatan 18
Vasastan ⑦
+46 (0)8 557 666 30
bliquebynobis.se/arc

If Korean *ssam*-style food, Asian drinks, and panoramic views tick all your boxes, then head to Arc restaurant on the top floor of hotel Blique by Nobis. Sit indoors during the colder months or find a seat on the terrace near the outdoor bar with a 360-degree view of Stockholm on long summer nights.

74 RÖDA HUSET
Malmskillnads-gatan 9
Norrmalm ①
+46 (0)8 480 043 97
rodahuset.nu

Röda Huset, which is located next to the city's most iconic roundabout in Sergels torg, is housed in an eye-catching, red building. Find a front-row row and gaze at the famous, 37-metre tall obelisk with 80.000 glass prisms while you sample superb drinks and delicious food.

75 HERMANS
Fjällgatan 23-B
Södermalm ⑤
+46 (0)8 643 94 80
hermans.se

If you're walking from Slussen along Katarinavägen, you will eventually end up in a hippie-like, green oasis with hammocks, colourful furniture, and stunning views of the city. Hermans has been a vegetarian institution since the 1990s, tantalising diners' taste buds with their planet-friendly buffets and homemade desserts.

The 5 best places to
EAT WITH THE LOCALS

---

76 PORTAL

Sankt Eriksplan 1
Vasastan ⑦
+46 (0)8 30 11 01
portalrestaurant.se

Portal is a chic and cosy local restaurant in Sankt Eriksplan. Its owner, Klas Lindberg, is an award-winning chef, who serves modern Swedish delicacies at reasonable prices. You'll find plenty of locals in this charming venue behind its arched windows every day, but they also have 12 drop-in seats at the bar for last-minute guests.

77 WOODSTOCKHOLM

Mosebacke torg 9
Södermalm ⑤
+46 (0)8 36 93 99
woodstockholm.com

At Woodstockholm, the menu changes often with dishes prepared according to specific themes. Each theme is extended in the decor, the music and the details, for an incredibly unique experience. An evening here is guaranteed to be memorable in the best of ways.

78 BABETTE

Roslagsgatan 6
Vasastan ⑦
+46 (0)8 509 022 24
babette.se

Babette is a tiny local place that is often crowded because their pizza is too good for words. You will find the daily pizza menu on the blackboard on the wall. Try their sharing platters and also their amazing selection of wines from interesting and original producers.

79 BRASSERIE GODOT

Grev Turegatan 36
Östermalm ②
+46 (0)8 660 06 14
godot.se

Year after year Brasserie Godot has succeeded in withstanding fads and trends while staying popular. The regulars tend to be more middle-aged during the week and younger on weekends – but the mood is always great. The owners gave their friend, the artist Eric Ericson, free rein to decorate the walls, windows, light fixtures, and plates.

80 AGNES

Norra Agnegatan 43
Kungsholmen ⑧
+46 (0)8 410 470 19
restaurangagnes.com

Visiting Agnes is like coming home to a hospitable friend from Southern Europe. The food is mainly Mediterranean but also has influences from other parts of the world. The waiters are knowledgeable and familiar, the atmosphere at the long tables is relaxed and the selection of wines that are served by the glass is generous.

76 PORTAL

5

SMALL *and* SPECIAL

places to eat

---

81 **LILLA EGO**
Västmannagatan 69
Vasastan ⑦
+46 (0)8 27 44 55
lillaego.com

A visit to Lilla Ego is a must, but do book months in advance. Otherwise, just hope that you are super-lucky to get a seat at the bar. This elegant place is every Stockholmer's hidden gem. The food, the service, the atmosphere, the prices… Everything here is amazing.

82 **PUNK ROYALE**
Folkungagatan 128
Södermalm ⑤
+46 (0)8 128 224 11
punkroyale.se

Punk Royale is the rebellious and ingenious younger brother of Stockholm's high-end fine dining places, a playful restaurant with high ambitions, side-stepping conventions. But the duo behind this controversial place know how to cook. Expect a lot of noise, humorous arrangements on the plates and an evening full of surprises.

83 **FRÄMMAT**
Dalagatan 54
Vasastan ⑦
+46 (7)6 835 35 52
frammat.com

This intimate, convivial eatery that oozes good vibes and great food is located further down the street. Främmat is run by two very experienced chefs, blending classic French cuisine with a more innovative, creative take on cuisine that doesn't believe in rules.

84 ETOILE

**Norra Stations-
gatan 51
Vasastan ⑦
+46 (0)8 10 10 70
*restaurantetoile.se***

The name Etoile is your first indication of the lofty ambitions of the chef of this little gem, which can seat 26. But they don't do pompous here. Instead, you're in for a fun, innovative, playful, and surprising experience. The complete set menu of 20 course is both affordable and highly memorable.

85 BORD

**Roslagsgatan 43
Vasastan ⑦
+46 (0)8 91 40 88
*bord.restaurant***

This cosy little hang-out on Roslagsgatan, with exciting taste combinations and interesting wines, is all the rage at the moment. Like so many other up-and-coming businesses on the Stockholm restaurant scene, Bord is run by a chef who has previously worked in Michelin-starred kitchens. Tip: try their four-course Saturday lunch.

5 places to visit for their
ATMOSPHERE

86 BISTRO MIRABELLE

Tulegatan 22
Vasastan ⑦
+46 (0)8 122 023 66
bistromirabelle.se

Vasastan is known as Stockholm's little Paris and in an anonymous part of Tulegatan, Bistro Mirabelle has rapidly become a fave with many locals when they are looking for somewhere more intimate to eat. The food is rustic and unpretentious presented, with a robust, French wine list. Bistro Mirabelle is the neighbourhood restaurant that everyone wished they lived next door to.

87 GAZZA

Hornsgatan 66
Södermalm ⑤
gazzasthlm.se

Cramped, cosy, carbonara... What's not to like? Gazza is a *spaghetteria* that isn't afraid of butter or carbs – and neither are its devoted guests. The hard-working, dedicated servers, the stylish decor, the fact that it's always crowded and open late make Gazza a great gathering place in Hornsgatan.

88 BLECK

AT: LILLA BLECKTORNS-
PARKEN
Katarina Bangata 68
Södermalm ⑤
restaurangbleck.se

Bleck is located next to one of Söder's smaller parks. This place serves trendy, ambitious yet affordable food and has outdoor seating that is both warm and enjoyable until November (thanks to heat lamps). The atmosphere is welcoming and, as they like to say, dogs, children and all sorts are welcome!

89 ARTILLERIET

AT: ARMÉMUSEUM
Artillerigatan 13
Östermalm ②
+46 (0)8 664 34 30
restaurangartilleriet.se

Artilleriet and its huge, sunny outdoor terrace must be one of Östermalm's best-kept secrets. Hard to find if you don't know where to look, but immensely popular among those who have already been introduced to it. During the colder months you take a seat indoors under the white stone arches, where you can enjoy brunch, lunch, coffee, dinner or a cocktail.

90 BANANAS

Skånegatan 47
Södermalm ⑤
bistrobananas.se

Let's go bananas! The yellow neon sign welcomes guests to this casual bistro with a vibrant mix of tastes and people. Neapolitan pizza makes up a large part of the menu, which also includes some small dishes and snacks. The walk-in policy attracts a fun crowd and during summer the outdoor terrace is always buzzing.

The 5 best places for a traditional
FIKA

---

91 TÖSSEBAGERIET
Karlavägen 77
Östermalm ②
+46 (0)8 662 24 30
tosse.se

Tösse is a classic bakery and pastry shop that opened in 1920. Typical architectural features like the stucco ceiling have been beautifully preserved and they still uphold their philosophy of only using quality ingredients. But despite its history, Tösse is also innovative. For example, they invented the famous *semmelwrapen,* which is a new take on the classic Swedish sweetroll.

92 HAGA TÅRTCOMPANI & BAGERI
Torsgatan 75
Vasastan ⑦
+46 (0)8 19 34 34
hagabageri.se

This is a great place to stop for coffee or tea, with lovely pastries, homemade biscuits or a slice of one of the beautiful cakes. In addition to classic pastries like princess cake and cinnamon buns they also bake sweets with a modern twist and offer both gluten and lactose-free options.

93 RITORNO
Odengatan 80
Vasastan ⑦
+46 (0)8 32 01 06
ritorno.se

In the heart of Vasastan, old-fashioned patisserie Ritorno has treated several generations to coffee and sweets. This classic Stockholm cafes continues to attract a crowd of all ages and on sunny days the generous outdoor seating area with views of leafy Vasaparken is always full.

94 VETE-KATTEN

Kungsgatan 55
Norrmalm ①
+46 (0)8 20 84 05
vetekatten.se

If you want to enjoy an 18th-century-style Swedish version of afternoon tea, head to Vete-Katten, one of Stockholm's few remaining authentic patisseries. Here you can still enjoy a traditional *fika*, in a maze of corridors and rooms with embroidered lace cloths and old porcelain. The hidden courtyard is a glorious place to sit on sunny days.

95 BLÅ PORTEN

Djurgårdsvägen 64
Djurgården ⑥
+46 (0)8 663 87 59
blaporten.com

Blå Porten, which opened in 2016, is a local favourite. The blue-tiled entrance explains the name and the interior has been tastefully restored and preserved in consultation with an antiques dealer. The Italian-inspired garden provides a beautiful Mediterranean oasis to enjoy some sweet pastries after touring the nearby museums.

5 restaurants with
AMAZING INTERIORS

96 LUZETTE

AT: CENTRALSTATION
Centralplan 25
Norrmalm ①
+46 (0)8 519 316 00
luzette.se

A large part of the interior of modern brasserie Luzette, in the heart of the bustling central station, which dates from 1871, has been preserved as is. Designer Jonas Bohlin decorated it with mainly Swedish materials like limestone tiles, brass, wooden details and of course, his iconic ceiling lamps for Örsjö in a unique, cobalt blue version.

100 **BISTRO LEOPARDEN**

97 MATBAREN

AT: GRAND HÔTEL
**Södra Blasieholms-
hamnen 6**
Norrmalm ②
+46 (0)8 679 35 84
mdghs.se/matbaren

When Matbaren opened in 2007, British Studioilse was commissioned to create the interior. Even today, the decoration is still inspiring due to its mix of Scandinavian heritage and modern, global influences. Swedish primitive pieces from the 1700s are combined with contemporary lamps and furniture.

98 HILLENBERG

Humlegårdsgatan 14
Östermalm ②
+46 (0)8 519 421 53
hillenberg.se

Hillenberg has a mature vibe combining good food with good architecture. The wave-shaped room separators in blasted aluminium and the patterned marble floor designed by Okidoki! Arkitekter are just two of its eye-catching features.

99 BRASSERIE ASTORIA

Nybrogatan 15
Östermalm ②
+46 (0)8 20 85 81
brasserieastoria.com

Originally built as a cinema, Astoria has since undergone a bit of a redesign. This enormous, two-storey restaurant can serve hundreds of guests and has several spaces with different moods. The common dramatic theme throughout is a reference to its cinematic heritage, of course. Depending on where you're seated, you'll get to experience a different set design every time you visit.

100 BISTRO LEOPARDEN

Tegnérgatan 16
Norrmalm ①
+46 (0)70 480 13 22
bistroleoparden.se

Is Bistro Leoparden the world's best-looking pizzeria? Possibly. Here they serve Neapolitan pizza and other dishes, amid a decoration scheme of pink-tiled walls, apricot-painted ceilings, and cobalt-blue furniture. Enjoy the gorgeous colour clash while you eat!

The 5 nicest
GARDEN CAFES

---

101 ROSENDALS TRÄDGÅRD

**Rosendals-
terrassen 12
Djurgården** ⑥
+46 (0)8 545 812 70
rosendalstradgard.se

Rosendals Trädgård is often described as a must during summer, but in fact it is a lovely place all year around. Visit this beautiful market garden during harvest market in early autumn, in spring or in winter when the greenhouse is decorated with wreaths, Christmas flowers, green spruces and candles.

102 GAMLA ORANGERIET

AT: BERGIANSKA TRÄDGÅRDEN
**Veit Wittrocks väg 7
Norra Djurgården** ⑨
+46 (0)8 612 09 59
gamlaorangeriet.se

This old orangerie is located in Bergius Botanic Garden. Its many windows emit a soft glow on rainy days but they also have a lovely terrace. This organic cafe is the perfect spot for a meal, a sandwich, something sweet from their artisanal bakery or a place to relax and enjoy nature.

103 SLOTTSTRÄDGÅRDEN ULRIKSDAL

**Slottsträdgårds-
vägen 8
Solna** ⑨
+46 (0)8 514 822 30
rappne.se

You'll find another beautiful garden near Ulriksdal Palace. Here you can stroll for hours among nurseries, vegetable gardens and greenhouses. Pop into the garden cafe if you feel hungry. Visit the fields during harvest to pick your own flowers, onions, fresh herbs and root vegetables.

104 ZETAS TRÄDGÅRD

Blombacken 2
Segeltorp
+46 (0)8 525 297 00
zetas.se

If you feel up for a short excursion, then head to this verdant oasis where you can find Sweden's largest assortment of garden plants as well as containers, furnishings and interior decoration. There's also a garden cafe, with Finnish-Japanese inspired architecture, where you can sit down with a coffee or some homemade cakes, a sandwich or lunch.

105 VINTERVIKENS TRÄDGÅRD

Vinterviksvägen 30
Aspudden ④
+46 (0)70 441 61 58
vinterviken.com

Vintervikens Trädgård is located just a few underground stops to the southwest of Stockholm's inner city. Once you have taken in the atmosphere and have tried something from the environmentally-conscious cafe, you should take a walk around the area and see the buildings that used to be Alfred Nobel's dynamite factory.

102 GAMLA ORANGERIET

The 5 best places for
SWEDISH SWEETS

---

106 LAKRITSROTEN

Sveavägen 107
Vasastan ⑦
+46 (0)8 411 58 15
lakritsroten.se

The Swedes discovered liquorice in the late 1800s and since then it has become very popular. Salmiak, liquorice flavoured with salty ammonium chloride, especially is a favourite in the Nordic countries. At Sveavägen the liquorice root has its own specialist store with over 700 products.

108 GAMLA STANS POLKAGRISKOKERI

107 PÄRLANS KONFEKTYR

Nytorgsgatan 38
Södermalm ⑤
+46 (0)8 660 70 10
parlanskonfektyr.se

You must stop at Pärlans if you decide to take a stroll around Nytorget. In fact, it is even worth a detour. The people working at this lovely sweet shop wear thirties retro uniforms, play jazz tunes and cook the most delicious caramels in classic flavours and seasonal combinations. All is packed in cute boxes.

108 GAMLA STANS POLKAGRISKOKERI

Stora Nygatan 44
Gamla stan ③
+46 (0)8 10 71 82
*gamlastanspolkagris
kokeri.se*

Visit Gamla Stans Polkagriskokeri for some unique Swedish candy. The traditional red and white *polkagris* candy stick is peppermint flavoured and was invented in Sweden back in 1859. This charming shop sells colourful handmade candy sticks, caramels, lollipops and you can peek into the kitchen and see them boil the sweets.

109 KRÜMEL

Valhallavägen 53
Vasastan ⑦
+46 (0)72 152 32 25
krumelcookies.com

Stockholm's first shop for crunchy cookies is called Krümel. Kaja, its founder, admits it takes a lot of self-restraint on her behalf not to tuck into the cookie dough all day. The hand-rolled cookies are baked until gooey inside with a crispy surface. Enjoy the cookies on site or take some to go in a cute little box.

110 INGRID

Regeringsgatan 91
Norrmalm ①
+46 (0)8 411 58 50

Ingrid is a bit of a family affair. Today it's run by second-generation bun baker Julia Holknekt, who took over from her mother. Their vanilla buns are worth a detour and if you arrive early in the morning, you might even be able to score one that's still hot, straight from the oven.

5 of the best
BAKERIES

---

111 LILLEBRORS

Rörstrandsgatan 10
Vasastan ⑦
lillebrors.se

This tiny artisan bakery sells divine buns, bread and pastries. Their sourdough bread is baked with organic emmer wheat, which gives this nutritious bread its unique taste. On weekends, the locals queue here for breakfast buns. Do try their Swedish crispbread, it is delicious.

112 GREEN RABBIT

Tegnérgatan 17
Vasastan ⑦
+46 (0)8 20 46 26
mdghs.se/green-rabbit

In a sense, Green Rabbit is an experimental workshop for developing and preserving Swedish bread culture. They do use rye, but they also experiment with older and different flours. Enjoy a soup lunch and Swedish varieties on sandwiches or take away freshly baked loaves or buns.

113 STORA BAGERIET

Sibyllegatan 2
Östermalm ②
+46 (0)8 27 72 72
storabageriet.com

Stora Bageriet prides itself on 300 years of history. While the bakers took a break here and there, this place is very much up and running again. When you stand near the cashier, you can watch them hard at work in the bakery. It's hard to resist their artisan bread and pastries.

114 ROBIN DELSELIUS BAGERI

Renstiernas gata 19
Södermalm ⑤
+46 (0)8 408 016 15
robindelseliusbageri.se

Many Stockholmers cheered when Robin Delselius, a third-generation baker, opened the doors to his bakery at Södermalm. The Delselius family has had bakeries in the archipelago for several decades, but this is the first in town. Here they sell homemade and organic bread and the interior strikes the perfect balance between timeless and classic.

115 LES PETITS BOUDINS

Fridhemsgatan 60
Kungsholmen ⑧
+46 (0)8 650 48 50

Les Petits Boudins is hidden near the intersection of Fridhemsgatan and Alströmergatan, just a few steps from busy Sankt Eriksgatan. This place has a cosy neighbourhood feel, with heavenly stone-baked sourdough bread and French jazz on the sound system. Tip: on Sundays, the bakers take the day off so be sure to visit this place on weekdays or Saturdays.

114 ROBIN DELSELIUS BAGERI

The 5 best places for
ICE CREAM

---

116 FRYST

**Kungsholms
strand 167
Kungsholmen** ⑧
+46 (0)8 653 80 98
fryst.net

You can find this small ice-cream bar near Karlberg Castle by following the queue that snakes its way along the façade. The shop started out as a hole in the wall but has since expanded, adding some seats. Taste as many flavours as you like and order half-scoops if you find it difficult to choose.

117 SNÖ

**Odengatan 92
Vasastan** ⑦
+46 (0)8 32 30 10
snogelateria.se

Gelateria Snö (meaning snow in Swedish) is located next to Vasaparken. Don't let the queue scare you off! Their creamy gelato is worth the wait. Why don't you pick your flavour while you wait? They offer several unique ones – including cucumber, mint and melon or burnt butter and rosemary.

118 TRIPPLE OH! ICE CREAM

**Nybrogatan 23
Östermalm** ②
+46 (0)8 664 40 00
ooo.se

Interested in tasting some experimental ice cream that was inspired by Nordic nature? Head to the artisan ice-cream cafe in Nybrogatan to find out what some truly unique combinations like cucumber and aquavit, rapeseed and lemon or goat milk and redcurrants taste like.

119 KUNGSHOLMENS GLASSFABRIK

Pipersgatan 14
Kungsholmen ⑧
+46 (0)8 650 58 04
kungsholmens
glassfabrik.se

This ice-cream shop is a hidden secret among 'Kungsholmers'. Most people are not inclined to stop here unless they've heard about it. Do pop in to taste one of their tasty ice creams or cooling sorbets in seasonal flavours, made from only the finest ingredients. Take a seat outside, overlooking the leafy baroque garden of Piperska Muren.

120 GLASSVERKSTAN

Slupskjulsvägen 28-B
Skeppsholmen ⑥
glassverkstan.se

Sitting on the quayside with an ice cream in hand, watching boats glide by on the glittering water to the sound of lapping waves – can you think of anything better? Probably not. Glassverkstan sells Skeppshomlen's smoothest ice cream. Tip: If you're lucky, you'll run into their vintage ice-cream truck when you walk across the bridge to the island. They serve their gelato there as well.

118 TRIPLE OH! ICE CREAM

BRÄNNERIAN

45 PLACES FOR A DRINK

The 5 best
COFFEE SHOPS

---

121 **JOHAN & NYSTRÖM**
   Swedenborgsgatan 7
   Södermalm ⑤
   +46 (0)70 790 48 35
   johanochnystrom.se

In 2004 Johan & Nyström opened and since then, they have transformed Sweden as a coffee-drinking nation. With their high-quality, gently roasted and fair-trade coffees and teas they have raised consumer awareness by organising courses and selling their products and equipment in several cafes and coffee bars. Visit their concept store!

122 **LYKKE COFFEE BAR**
   Nytorgsgatan 38
   Södermalm ⑤
   lykkenytorget.se

The coffee in your cup at Lykke comes from their own coffee farms, without intermediaries. In addition to serving delicious food and good coffee which you can drink with a clear conscience, this bright, colourful coffee bar is a really pleasant hang-out with a nice atmosphere.

123 DROP COFFEE

**Wollmar
Yxkullsgatan 10
Södermalm** ⑤
+46 (0)70 777 94 88
dropcoffee.com

Are you a coffee connoisseur who values quality and craftsmanship? Then head to Drop Coffee next to Mariatorget, where you will find like-minded friends who take coffee drinking very seriously. This place roasts its own organic and fair-trade coffee, serving it in a variety of ways – both cold brewed and hot.

124 MELLQVIST KAFFEBAR

**Rörstrandsgatan 4
Vasastan** ⑦
+46 (0)8 30 23 80

Mellqvist Kaffebar is always at the top of the list when Stockholmers are asked to rate their favourite cafes. Everyone who steps through the door of this crowded, cosy place is given the same warm welcome as the regulars. On summer days, the seats along the brick wall are the perfect spot for people-watching.

125 CRUM HEAVEN

**Högbergsgatan 38-40
Södermalm** ⑤

Crum Heaven is an art space cum coffee joint. Although they call themselves an espresso bar, you can definitely get more here than some bean elixir. The menu includes breakfast, sandwiches, salads, and Swedish potato pancakes with sweet and savoury toppings. Indulge in a delightful caffeine break while you take in the captivating art exhibitions.

5 great
NATURAL WINE BARS

---

126 VINA
Sofiagatan 1
Södermalm ⑤
+46 (0)76 581 32 74
vina.nu

Don't go to Vina for classics as this place mainly serves natural wines from other regions. If you're hungry, then just order a plate of *pintxos,* cheeses, cold cuts or any of the delicious dishes on the menu. Weather permitting, you can sit outside with a view of Greta Garbo square.

127 SAVANT BAR
Tegnérgatan 4
Norrmalm ①
+46 (0)76 021 26 30
savantbar.se

Savant rapidly gained a loyal following. Their wine selection veers towards the natural, is comprehensive (more than 500 wines on the menu), and they add new bottles every week. At this small bar, they prioritise small-scale production with a sustainable approach and their organic vegetable-based menu is equally planet-friendly.

128 AMBAR

Tomtebogatan 22
Vasastan ⑦
+46 (0)73 158 51 53
ambarvinbar.se

Orange wines takes pride of place on the menu here, as well as other drinks that lean towards the oxidised – basically anything that's amber. Stockholmers were quick to discover Ambar, loving its homey, unpretentious, cosy feel. The small Japanese dishes on the menu contain pickled and fermented ingredients – a perfect match for the orange wines.

129 GEMLA

Magnus Ladulåsgatan 8-D
Södermalm ⑤
+46 (0)73 339 73 27
gemlavinbar.se

Gemla stands for genuine craftsmanship – this fetching natural wine bar is also a furniture workshop. The wine list focuses entirely on artisanal wines – from unsprayed vines and without unnecessary additives. The price is also quite affordable, giving you the opportunity to taste different bottles.

130 NEKTAR

Rörstrandsgatan 12
Vasastan ⑦
+46 (0)8 771 14 70
nektarstockholm.com

Nektar proves that size doesn't matter. Founders Embla Brorsson and Eric Seger have an impressive, combined track record and Nektar fulfils their dream of opening a small natural wine bar and mini bistro of their own. Its location at Rörstrandsgatan is especially lovely during summertime when the quarter turns into a pedestrian zone.

The 5 best places serving
CRAFT BEER

---

131 KATARINA ÖLKAFÉ

Katarina Bangata 27
Södermalm ⑤
katarinaolkafe.se

Over the years, beer pub Katarina Ölkafé has filled plenty of bellies with their homemade pastrami on rye and reuben sandwiches. What about the drinks? Well, they call it a beer cafe for a reason. Here you find everything from local microbreweries to a carefully curated selection of bottles from around the world.

132 PANG PANG FESTAURANG

Långholmsgatan 34
Södermalm ④
+45 (0)76 016 01 23
pangpangbrewery.se

Stockholm's first craft beer microbrewery in Hökarängen had outgrown its premises, prompting a move into town. Apart from their fun and creative label design (and good beer of course), they are also known for their festive weekend brunches and a seasoned kitchen team who know exactly how to cure your hangovers with some salty, fatty taste sensations.

133 RACAMACA

Wollmar
Yxkullsgatan 5-B
Södermalm ⑤
racamaca.com

Racamaca is a cosy culinary gem, delighting guests with delectable Scandinavian-Mediterranean fusion dishes. They partnered with micro-brewery Gröna Linjen Bryggeri to serve mouth-watering ales and host popular brewing events, inviting guests to partake in the creation of new, exciting beer experiments.

134 OMNIPOLLOS HATT

Hökens gata 1-A
Södermalm ⑤
+46 (0)76 119 48 44
omnipolloshatt.com

The duo behind Omnipollos hatt started producing beer by developing their recipes at home and travelling to different breweries around the world to fine-tune their ales. Nowadays they run their own bar in Södermalm where beer fans can sample their famous brews. Tip: Take a trip to their brewery, Omnipollos kyrka, in an old church (!) in Sundbyberg.

135 OMAKA

Uggelviksgatan 2
Östermalm ①
+46 (0)8 400 504 40
omaka.beer

Hedda Spendrup is descended from one of Sweden's most established brewing families. With Omaka, she resolutely takes the family business into the future. Their brunches with DJ performances are popular and you can also take a tour of the brewery to learn more about the brewing process, followed by a tasting of their exciting beer.

5 bars serving
SMALL BITES

---

136 BAR AGRIKULTUR

Skånegatan 79
Södermalm ⑤
+46 (0)70 880 12 00
baragrikultur.com

At this cosy bar, guests can enjoy seasonal Swedish produce in a welcoming, open-kitchen ambience. Their salt brined cucumbers with smetana, honey and dill heads have become such a classic appetiser that Stockholmers now serve it at dinner parties. Book ahead or grab one of the seats at the bar for walk-ins.

140 BAR NINJA

137 BRÄNNERIAN

Folkungagatan 136
Södermalm ⑤
+46 (0)8 121 115 02
brannerian.se

Brännerian is a favourite haunt for gin lovers and the spirits they serve are produced in-house. Besides well-mixed cocktails, they also serve a few savoury snacks and grilled open sandwiches that pair perfectly with a gin & tonic.

138 SCHMALTZ BAR & DELICATESSEN

Nybrogatan 19
Östermalm ②
+46 (0)8 88 16 58
schmaltz.se

A spontaneous dinner, a mouthful of pickles or just an aperitif... Schmaltz has it all. This tiny and tasteful renovated bar and delicatessen serves sustainable dishes with international influences. Its Yiddish name, *shmalts*, means rendered chicken fat, and refers to its location in a building that used to be a Jewish school.

139 RÅDHUSBAREN

Bergsgatan 23
Kungsholmen ⑧
+46 (0)70 845 63 36

This under-the-radar-bar is one of Kungsholmen's best-kept secrets. A reasonably-priced neighbourhood hang-out with lovely staff, a homey feel, and dishes that served from the small open kitchen directly in the bar. This is a place for a more mature crowd. Don't be surprised to find yourself sitting next to some famous cultural figures or designers while you gorge on some oysters.

140 BAR NINJA

Katarina Bangata 29
Södermalm ⑤
barninja.se

A trendy hole-in-the-wall bar next to Nytorget, Bar Ninja serves wine from small-scale and natural producers, combining a festive atmosphere with tasty fare. On Wednesdays they sell bread from Dåndimpens bakery (also a tip but located in the more inaccessible south of town).

5 amazing
ROOFTOP
drinking spots

---

141 **TAK STOCKHOLM**

Brunkebergstorg 4
Norrmalm ①
+46 (0)8 587 220 80
tak.se

High up above Stockholm, TAK offers fantastic views. As its name suggests (*tak* means roof in Swedish), this bar is located on top of a hotel building next to Brunkebergstorg in Norrmalm. Besides its great terrace, TAK has a superb Asian restaurant.

142 **SPESSO**

Malmskillnads-
gatan 38-B
Norrmalm ①
+46 (0)8 480 043 98
spesso.se

Elegant Italian restaurant Spesso has panoramic windows and is open year-round. During the warmer months, they also have a lush, delightful outdoor bar called Tetto. From here you have a view of the Djurgården waterfront, the nearby Hötorget skyscrapers, and the iconic NK clock.

143 **URBAN DELI**
9TH FLOOR

Sveavägen 44
Norrmalm ①
+46 (0)8 425 500 02
urbandeli.org/
sveavagen

Stockholm doesn't have that many roof terraces, so Urban Deli's rooftop bar was a welcome feature in the city when it was built. Leave bustling Sveavägen behind and take the lift to the ninth floor. This bar is a green art park with sculptures and amazing views.

144 DRAMATEN-TERRASSEN

AT: KUNGLIGA
DRAMATISKA TEATERN
Nybrogatan 2
Östermalm ②
+46 (0)8 665 62 66
dramaten
restaurangerna.se

The sun-drenched terrace of The Royal Dramatic Theatre attracts both Stockholmers and tourists. The terrace is open in the summertime and easy to find as you walk through the theatre's golden entrance doors. From this front-row spot, you have a perfect view of Stockholm's most glamorous quarters and the glittering water of Nybroviken.

145 SÖDER

Hornsgatan 18
Södermalm ⑤
+46 (0)8 527 756 10
freyjasoder.se/soder

Discover Söder, a captivating rooftop terrace with two fantastic bars, a sausage kiosk, and breath-taking views of Stockholm. As the sun sets over the shacks and cobblestones, enjoy a variety of cocktails, wines, and beers, as well as Söder's romantic charm. Tip: Its main restaurant Freyja serves delectable culinary creations.

143 URBAN DELI 9TH FLOOR

5
COCKTAIL BARS
not to miss

---

146 TJOGET
Hornsbruksgatan 24
Södermalm ④
+46 (0)8 22 00 21
tjoget.com

Tjoget is a restaurant, bar, and wine bodega, where craftsmanship is a top priority. Taste one of their flavoursome cocktails, which are inspired by Southern Europe, Northern Africa, and the Middle East and you'll immediately understand why they are one of the world's top 50 cocktail bars.

147 PARADISO
Timmermans-gatan 24
Södermalm ⑤
+46 (0)8 720 61 51
paradisostockholm.se

Paradiso's Caribbean look and feel was inspired by Miami and Cuba. Besides well-mixed classic rum-cocktails and signature drinks such as their own 'Channel Orange' with dark rum, fortified wine, coconut, carrot, nutmeg, and absinthe, they also serve a nice selection of plant-based dishes.

148 A BAR CALLED GEMMA
Grev Turegatan 30
Östermalm ②
+46 (0)70-584 50 90
abarcalledgemma.se

Appearances can be deceiving – this bar, which is located in a former seventies-style bank building with its modest interior, might sound a bit dull – but here the drinks speak for themselves. The skill behind each delicately mixed drink makes A Bar Called Gemma one of the capital's most interesting drinking spots.

149 CORNER CLUB

Lilla Nygatan 16
Gamla stan ③
+46 (0)8 20 85 83
cornerclub.se

The Old Town has certainly stepped up its game in terms of bars and restaurants – you can find some of Stockholm's most pleasant bars hidden among the tourist traps. Corner Club is one of them, changing its drink menu on a seasonal basis, but rest assured, you'll always be served interesting flavour sensations and classics with a twist.

150 LUCY'S FLOWER SHOP

Birger Jarlsgatan 20
Östermalm ①
lucysstockholm.se

Lucy's Flower Shop is a real hidden secret. Passers-by tend to overlook the anonymous door in Birger Jarlsgatan. You need to know what awaits behind it and walk down the stairs into the basement where you will find, perhaps, the best cocktails in town. This speakeasy has only a few drinks on the menu, but what they serve is definitely in a league of its own!

146 TJOGET

The 5 best
WINE BARS

---

151 **COMBO VINBAREN**
   Odengatan 52
   Vasastan ⑦
   +46 (0)8 522 256 52
   combovinbaren.com

The team behind Stockholm favourites like Bistro Süd and PA & Co have opened a small wine bar next to the City Library. The wine menu features simple yet excellent wines as well as rare, precious bottles from all over the world. Do not miss their signature dessert called the 'Gino', which was invented in the nineties.

154 TYGE & SESSIL

152 GRUS GRUS

Karlbergsvägen 14
Vasastan ⑦
+46 (0)8 610 66 00
grusgrusvinbaren.se

Grus Grus is the wine bar of restaurant Tranan. It serves wines from small-scale, for the most part organic producers, with an emphasis on natural winemaking. Tip: enquire about the bottles from Tranan's famous 'secret' wine cellar, which are not listed on the menu.

153 ALBA VINBAR

Skånegatan 88
Södermalm ⑤
+46 (0)8 36 96 50
albavinbar.se

We could have also added Alba to our list of natural wine bars, with its selection of artisanal wines – from lively, carbonated sparklers to rich, terroir-driven gems. Patrons love the hip hop beats, hand-written notes, and warm welcome. Here the motto is quite simple: wine should always be a joyous adventure.

154 TYGE & SESSIL

Brahegatan 4
Östermalm ②
+46 (0)8 519 422 77
tygesessil.se

Natural wine is the new buzzword and the Tyge & Sessil wine cafe picked up on this trend. Enjoy lesser-known grape varieties grown by small-scale, artisanal winemakers, that accurately reflect the growing conditions of that particular year. The laidback atmosphere and interesting wine list will appeal to everyone with an appetite for new discoveries.

155 FOLII

Erstagatan 21
Södermalm ⑤
folii.se

This is a tiny, hidden gem for visitors who like to hang out with locals. Folii is run by two experienced sommeliers, Jonas Sandberg and Béatrice Becher, and they change the menu and wine list daily. They do not take reservations, so just stop by and enjoy savoury snacks and delectable drinks.

5 nice places for a
DRINK IN THE SUN

---

156 MÄLARPAVILJONGEN

Norr Mälarstrand 64
Kungsholmen ⑧
+46 (0)8 650 87 01
malarpaviljongen.se

This lush oasis with stunning views across the waters of Riddarfjärden offers a rainbow-coloured welcome to everybody. The cafe and the pavilion were built in the forties but since then, Mälarpaviljongen has expanded with three flowery floating docks on Lake Mälaren. A perfect spot to eat, drink and watch boats sail by.

157 KAJSAS I PARKEN

AT: VITABERGSPARKEN
Stora Mejtens
Gränd 16
Södermalm ⑤
+46 (0)76 044 45 41
kajsas.se

Kajsas i Parken is located in Vitabergsparken in the eastern part of Södermalm. Although the surrounding environment is quiet and green, this popular summer bar becomes a colourful place to hang out with friends, whether you are in the mood for some coffee, or prefer cocktails, wine or beer.

158 BOULEBAR TANTO

Tantogatan 85
Södermalm ⑤
+46 (0)10 162 92 00
boulebar.se

Do you fancy some *petanque* and cuisine from the Midi in France? Boulebar wants to get more people to discover the magic of this game. One of their bars in Stockholm is located at Hornstulls strand in Tantolunden. Why not sip a glass of pastis while getting your game on?

159 **MOSEBACKE-TERRASSEN**
AT: SÖDRA TEATERN
Mosebacke torg 1-3
Södermalm ⑤
+46 (0)8 531 993 79
sodrateatern.com/
mosebacketerrassen

This biergarten in Södra Teatern, in the heart of the bohemian Södermalm neighbourhood, is a vibrant outdoor hotspot for socialising and for enjoying live performances. Go to the smaller Södra Bar or Champagnebaren if you prefer breathtaking views over the capital in a more intimate setting.

160 **EDEN**
Smedsuddsvägen 23
Kungsholmen ⑧
+46 (0)8 84 80 77
edensthlm.se

In the summertime, Eden is a popular hang-out, serving Mediterranean-inspired food and drinks, with people flocking here for the music and the great ambiance. It is located in a turn-of-the-century villa at Smedsudden, a peninsula on Kungsholmen, offering glorious views of the water, boats and Västerbron. On warm summer evenings, Eden really lives up to its name.

158 BOULEBAR TANTO

5
CIDER FACTORIES
worth visiting

---

161 **VÄRMDÖ MUSTERI**
   Eknäsvägen 25
   Ingarö
   +46 (0)70 857 12 00
   varmdomusteri.se

Värmdö Musteri is run by a Swedish-Danish couple who sell their award-winning apple juice, homegrown produce like jelly, jam, apple pies and Danish smørrebrød in their cafe and farm shop. You can also book a guided tour and see how apples are transformed into must, vinegar, cider and calvados.

162 LIDINGÖ MUSTERI

Grönsta Prästgård 8
Lidingö
+46 (0)70 524 83 05
lidingomusteri.se

People bring their own garden apples here to be pressed. Enjoy a *fika* with buns and bread from Lidingö Bröd & Pâtisserie and coffee from a local roastery while you are waiting. Lidingö is a lovely destination for a day trip to nature and the archipelago just around the corner.

163 EDSVIKENS MUSTERI

Sollentunavägen 55
Sollentuna
+46 (0)73 639 02 23
edsvikensmusteri.se

The idea for Edsvikens Musteri was born when two women realised there had to be a way of processing all the apples from people's gardens. Today they have a small-scale, craft-like production plant where they press garden apples into a delicious apple must.

164 ÄPPELFABRIKEN

Viksundsvägen 60
Svartsjö
appelfabriken.se

Äppelfabriken has one of the country's oldest apple farms dating back to the 17th century. Take a stroll in the apple orchard, enjoy homemade cider and a *fika* baked with organic ingredients. Svartsjö is located on Färingsö, an island in Lake Mälaren, which you can reach by car.

165 ROSENHILL

Nyckelbyvägen 22
Ekerö
+46 (0)8 560 200 60
rosenhill.nu

Rosenhill is a farm in Ekerö using organic methods to grow apples, among other things. The laidback, hippie atmosphere makes this a great place to chill and enjoy the Swedish countryside. During the growing season you can pick herbs and vegetables to take home, make your own apple cider, enjoy homemade food or buy arts and crafts.

90 PLACES
TO SHOP

The 5 best
FLOWER SHOPS

166 CHRISTOFFERS BLOMMOR

Kåkbrinken 10
Gamla stan ③
+46 (0)8 24 00 75
christoffersblommor.se

Christoffer Broman and his team enchant the locals with wonderfully wild bouquets and styled flowers for the fashion industry. It all started in the early 2000s with a miniature shop in a narrow alley in Gamla stan where Christoffer himself still creates his natural arrangements.

170 BLADVERKET

167 IN BLOOM

Östgötagatan 22
Södermalm Ⓢ
+46 (0)70 770 22 71
inbloom.nu

In Bloom is a tiny but oh so lovely flower shop. Sassa Lee, who runs it, has a loyal fanbase in the neighbourhood and the atmosphere is very intimate and personal. Behind the shop there is a secret studio where she occasionally holds flower arranging and other events.

168 FLORABAREN

Birger Jarlsgatan 35
Norrmalm Ⓝ
+46 (0)8 406 88 30
florabarenstockholm.se

Florabaren is primarily a flower shop, but you can also go there for a glass of bubbly or a cup of coffee and then buy a lovely flower arrangement to take home. This pink-walled place also sells a wide range of dried flowers.

169 FLORISTKOMPANIET

Norrlandsgatan 16
Norrmalm Ⓝ
+46 (0)8 678 14 19
floristkompaniet.se

This lush, centrally located oasis specialises in creating beautifully unruly, sprawling bouquets with seasonal flowers. The shop's interior is also inspiring and they have a cute selection of delicate ceramics, handmade cards and botanical beauty products, making this a good spot to pick up last-minute gifts.

170 BLADVERKET

Nytorgsgatan 23-A
Södermalm
+46 (0)8 644 58 77
bladverket.se

Locals would probably prefer to keep this deliciously pretty florist a secret. Since 1992, Bladverket in Nytorgsgatan has created brilliant bunches of blooms. The variety is huge here, with bridal bouquets and corsages to table decorations and wreaths. The number of returning customers speaks for itself.

5 great shops for
SWEDISH DENIM

171 WEEKDAY

Drottninggatan 63
Norrmalm ①
+46 (0)8 411 29 70
weekday.com

Weekday is a contemporary streetwear and denim brand, drawing inspiration from Scandinavian style and offering a wide range of jeans models in organic cotton at really reasonable prices. There are Weekday stores at two locations in Stockholm: Götgatan in Södermalm and Drottninggatan in the city centre.

172 NUDIE

Skånegatan 75
Södermalm ⑤
+46 (0)10 151 57 15
nudiejeans.com

Swedish clothing brand Nudie specialises in raw and prewashed denim jeans. You can find all their models and colours in their store in Skånegatan, and they also offer free repairs. As part of their ambition to achieve sustainable consumption patterns, they only use 100% organic cotton denim for their jeans.

173 JEANERICA

AT: NK DEPARTMENT STORE
Hamngatan 18-20
Norrmalm ①
+46 (0)8 762 81 91
nk.se

Jeanerica is a play on jeans and America. This Swedish denim brand was founded by two industry veterans who wanted to re-create the classic American blue jeans in a contemporary Nordic style. The result is a collection that is seasonless, ageless and organic.

174 ACNE STUDIOS

Norrmalmstorg 2
Norrmalm ②
+46 (0)8 611 64 11
acnestudios.com

Acne Studios is a fashion house with a multidisciplinary approach creating everything from ready-to-wear to magazines but it all started with jeans in 1996. This store used to be a former bank building where the Stockholm Syndrome heist took place in 1973. Here you'll find denim in different styles. The changing rooms are in the old bank vault.

175 DR DENIM

Bondegatan 46
Södermalm ⑤
+46 (0)76 863 76 87
drdenim.com

Two brothers and their father founded Dr. Denim 2004 in Gothenburg. They dreamt of creating denim rooted in the present, that spanned several seasons with a traditional design. The company is still a family business and in their Stockholm store in SoFo you can browse their range of slim, straight, flared and cropped denim.

172 NUDIE

5 shops for
SWEDISH
JEWELLERY DESIGN

―――――――――

176 BLUE BILLIE

Södermannagatan 27
Södermalm ⑤
+46 (0)8 29 94 66
bluebillie.com

Daniela Upmark's jewellery brand was a trendsetter from the start. Their popular range of letter necklaces was soon expanded with fashionable pearls, edgy chains and various symbols, hoops and rings in gold, silver, and diamonds. Shop to add to your own jewellery collection or browse for gifts that are oh-so-thoughtful.

177 WOS

Gamla Brogatan 27
Norrmalm ①
+46 (0)8 616 00 16
wosstore.com

Looking for some avantgarde accessories? Head to Wos in Gamla Brogatan or Hornsgatan where you can score some unique and personalised jewellery from exciting emerging Swedish designers or their own brands Wos and Wos up. The range also includes sunglasses, head-gear, and handbags. Each piece makes a bold statement.

178 ALL BLUES

Birger Jarlsgatan 2
Östermalm ②
+46 (0)8 402 09 21
allblues.se

All Blues was founded by two friends, Fredrik Nathorst and Jacob Skragge. They gained a lot of attention for their unisex line and clean aesthetic, both at home and internationally. Every piece is handmade by expert artisans in an old foundry outside of Stockholm. You can shop their All Blues jewellery collection in their flagship store.

179 MARIA NILSDOTTER

Mäster
Samuelsgatan 3
Östermalm ②
+46 (0)73 650 38 37
marianilsdotter.com

Claws, insects and aliens combined with pearls, jewels, silver, and gold... Maria Nilsdotter finds inspiration in fantasy worlds and fairy tales. Step into her imaginative, wistful, and magical universe in her intriguing dark boutique in Bibliotekstan to browse her timeless, yet punkish jewellery collections.

180 ENNUI ATELIER

AT: NK DEPARTMENT STORE
Hamngatan 18-20
Norrmalm ①
+46 (0)8 762 87 92
ennuiatelier.com

Say goodbye to boring plastic jewellery. At Ennui's luxurious piercing studio, you can treat your ears to new piercings and get beautiful gold and diamond jewellery on the spot! They practise single needle piercing and the whole experience is a treat. They also design rings, necklaces, and bracelets.

The 5 best
STATIONERY SHOPS

181 PEN STORE

Hornsgatan 98
Södermalm ⑤
+46 (0)8 515 102 50
penstore.se

Highlighters, brush pens and engravable pens are just some of the products you'll find at Pen Store. Visit the minimalistic shop and take a look at the iconic Ballograph desk set, which was widely used in banks and government agencies for several decades.

182 LAGERHAUS

Drottninggatan 31
Norrmalm ①
+46 (0)8 23 72 00
lagerhaus.se

Lagerhaus has a large range of affordable office stationery, which they design themselves. Funny quotes on notepads, pens in pastel hues, weekly planners and sparkling boxes… Plenty of cute desktop accessories you never knew you needed but which you probably cannot leave without.

183 PALMGRENS

Sibyllegatan 7
Östermalm ②
+46 (0)8 667 90 40
palmgrens.se

Palmgrens was established in 1896 when Stockholmers still got around by horse and buggy. Over the years, its product line has expanded from riding and horse equipment to include desk accessories, boxes and trunks made of vegetable-tanned leather. The store is still located in the same neighbourhood.

184 BOOKBINDERS DESIGN

Karlavägen 67
Östermalm ②
+46 (0)73 847 22 33
bookbindersdesign.com

Ever dreamt of your own personalised and unique stationery? At Bookbinders Design they specialise in quality-handcrafted notebooks, photo albums, diaries and boxes in a wide range of colours and shapes and many of them are available for embossing. Tip: it can take a few days to get something embossed so place your order in time.

185 STUDIO BARBARA BUNKE

Köpmangatan 10
Gamla stan ③
+46 (0)702 533 028
studiobarbarabunke.se

Barbara Bunke's shop, located in an 18th-century house, is one of Stockholm's few remaining paper shops. Barbara herself is an artist, designer and book-binder and advises her customers, surrounded by shelves of exclusive paper, handbound notebooks, rows of pens and dazzling cards.

5 must-visit
LIFESTYLE SHOPS

186 ARKET
Götgatan 36
Södermalm ⑤
arket.se

Take a break from bustling Söder and step into Arket's second branch in the capital, at the top of Götgatan's hill. Browse Scandi-chic interior design items and trendy garments. In their other, bigger store at Drottninggatan you can also find kids clothes and their Nordic-inspired cafe.

187 SINGULAR SOCIETY
Gamla Brogatan 28
Norrmalm ①
+46 (0)70 437 42 76
singular-society.com

Singular Society offers responsibly made life essentials of the highest possible quality. Thanks to an annual membership the brand can cut prices, mark-ups and guarantee full transparency. Europeans can also shop online but the sophisticated, minimalistic store is inspiring and definitely worth a visit.

188 APLACE
AT: BRUNO
SHOPPING CENTRE
Götgatan 36
Södermalm ⑤
+46 (0)8 643 31 10
aplace.com

Aplace was both a fashion magazine and a trade show before morphing into a store in 2007. Today their shop in Brunogallerian on top of Götgatsbacken carries clothes, accessories, shoes and interior objects by the most interesting Scandinavian brands and a well-curated secondhand-selection.

189 NITTY GRITTY

Krukmakargatan 26
Södermalm ⑤
+46 (0)8 658 24 40
nittygrittystore.com

Nitty Gritty was one of the first independent stores in Stockholm (1991) to sell carefully selected products from different brands, as a counter-reaction to all the mainline clothing department stores. Nowadays it still is a sure bet for exceptionally good fragrances, footwear, clothes and they also exhibit interesting contemporary art in the store.

190 GRANDPA

Södermannagatan 21
Södermalm ⑤
+46 (0)10 516 44 80
grandpastore.com

Think of a shop where functional and trendy outdoor brands are combined with Scandinavian interior design, organic soaps and useful books. That pretty much sums up Grandpa. Add a relaxed vibe and friendly staff and you will see why this old relative is worth a visit.

Stockholm's 5 most
FRAGRANT STORES

---

191 L:A BRUKET

Södermannagatan 19
Södermalm ⑤
+46 (0)8 615 00 11
labruket.se

The healing power of the Swedish west coast has been transported to the capital by L:a Bruket. This Varberg-based skincare brand only uses natural ingredients to develop products that are inspired by the Atlantic's salt, seaweed and water and which have traditionally been used in spa rituals for skin ailments.

195 FABLAB

192 BYREDO

Mäster
Samuelsgatan 6
Norrmalm ①
+46 (0)8 525 026 15
byredo.se

Byredo's boutique with its austere interior in a neutral colour palette perfectly matches the unisex fragrance line with its striking packaging design. The line also includes scented candles, soaps, skincare products (and leather goods). The understated fragrances capture memories, transforming them into scents.

193 STORA SKUGGAN

Östgötagatan 18
Södermalm ⑤
storaskuggan.com
collectandbottle.com

This Stockholm-based perfume studio sells its own, luxurious, handmade fragrances. You can also book a Collect & Bottle appointment at the store: browse a scent library of 80 carefully selected ingredients, create a unique formula, and blend your own fragrance to take home.

194 COW PARFYMERI

Norrlandsgatan 18
Norrmalm ①
+46 (0)8 611 15 04
cowparfymeri.se

COW is the go-to-place for professionals. This place only sells high-quality products and since its opening in 1999, the owners, Christian and Wenche Hughes, have scouted the world's best cosmetics brands for their store. The staff consist of experienced make-up artists who help you find the perfect products, and offer plenty of good advice.

195 FABLAB

Bondegatan 7
Södermalm ⑤
+46 (0)8 420 516 37
fab-lab.nu

At FABLAB, set designer and stylist Johan Svenson sells carefully curated interior design and beauty products. The store, in an old milk shop, carries a variety of unique niche perfume brands as well as exclusive home fragrances, scented candles, and hair and body care.

5 Swedish designed
ACCESSORY BRANDS

196 HESTRA

Norrlandsgatan 12
Norrmalm ①
+46 (0)8 678 77 10
hestragloves.se

At Hestra, the focus is on hands. For over 80 years, the family-owned company has been developing gloves to warm, protect, and provide comfort for your fingers in the most diverse environments. Their collection includes waterproof children's gloves, fashionable leather gloves, or ultra-functional but good-looking gloves for alpine sports and outdoor living.

197 HAPPY SOCKS

Mäster
Samuelsgatan 9
Norrmalm ①
+46 (0)8 611 87 02
happysocks.com

Since 2008, Happy Socks has spread happiness with its colourful, brilliantly patterned socks. Today they have concept stores worldwide, and several outlets in their hometown. The shop at Mäster Samuelsgatan was the first one they opened. Pop in to give this everyday accessory an update with dots, stripes or animal prints.

198 EOE EYEWEAR

Mäster
Samuelsgatan 10
Norrmalm ①
+46 (0)8 14 98 10
eoe-eyewear.com

The EoE eyewear brand pays tribute to its northern roots and has prioritised environmentally-conscious production from the start. In their flagship store you can buy beautifully designed sunglasses or try on different models from their line of specs, with names such as Jukkasjärvi, Hornavan and Abisko.

199 SANDQVIST

Götgatan 28
Södermalm ⑤
+46 (0)73 751 40 05
sandqvist.net

Engineer Anton Sandqvist was inspired by the Nordic landscape in combination with an urban city lifestyle when he sewed his first bag back in 2004. Nowadays Sandqvist is a well-known label and their functional cotton canvas backpacks and leather briefcases are worn by hipsters everywhere, from Scandinavia to large cities like Tokyo and Los Angeles.

200 EYTYS

Norrlandsgatan 22
Norrmalm ①
+46 (0)8 684 420 80
eytys.com

Having grown up with the street cultures of the eighties and nineties, two childhood friends – Jonathan Hirschfeld and Max Schiller – established sneaker brand Eytys in 2013. Their unisex line harks back to the golden era of sneakers and has taken the fashion world by storm with its thick, signature soles inspired by the deck shoes of the forties.

5 places to shop for **G I F T S** that will be appreciated

—————

201 TAMBUR

Folkungagatan 85
Södermalm ⑤
+46 (0)8 742 81 00
tamburstore.se

Tambur means 'hallway' in Swedish and the store reminds you of entering someone's home – albeit that you can buy everything here, from the homeware to the kitchen supplies, textiles and decorative objects. This is one of those shops that you want to move into, or at least not leave empty-handed.

202 THE MODERN STHLM

Nybrogatan 20
Östermalm ②
+46 (0)70 822 39 11
themodernsthlm.se

With a prime location in Nybrogatan, The Modern Sthlm invites you to step into a colourful and eclectic universe. Mother and daughter Camilla and Charlotte Ahlström run this shop together, selling a curated selection of unique, playful, modern European design. Glass objects, art, figurative tableware, interesting coffee table books – the place to find just the perfect gift for picky people with exquisite taste.

203 DESIGNTORGET

Sergelgatan 20
Norrmalm ①
+46 (0)8 758 75 20
designtorget.se

Designtorget has made a name for itself in the design world by offering a marketplace for form and innovation. They sell products by relatively unknown designers as well as established brands. Smaller furniture items, lamps, accessories, books and speakers... This is the perfect shop for anyone looking for something smart, functional and good-looking.

204 FOGELMARCK

Karlavägen 74
Östermalm ②
+46 (0)8 662 63 21
fogelmarck.se

Family-run Fogelmarck in Karlavägen is a perfect pitstop for presents. Fragrant candles and soaps, aesthetic board games, beautiful napkins, candle holders, decorative matchboxes – here you can find going-away gifts that most people will appreciate. They also sell a nice selection of furniture, lamps, and interior textiles.

205 ESTERIÖR

Äsögatan 144
Södermalm ⑤
+46 (0)8 121 591 00
www.esterior.se

Esteriör is an interior design studio and shop located in lovely SoFo, which sells colourful items with new and vintage playful shapes, with tons of personality. It's the kind of shop that you walk into and you immediately know that you'll walk out with something beautifully wrapped for the home of someone you love.

5 essential
FASHION SHOPS
for MEN

206 LUND & LUND

Sturegatan 12
Östermalm ②
+46 (0)8 661 07 35
lundochlund.se

Lund & Lund prides itself on gentleman's tailoring of the highest order. Before the two Lund brothers opened the shop in the mid-1900s, they had been sent to London and New York to learn pattern cutting. Today men of all ages still visit the shop to find the perfect outfit.

207 A DAY'S MARCH

Kungsgatan 3
Norrmalm ①
+46 (0)8 611 00 20
adaysmarch.com

Centrally located in Kungsgatan, A Day's March is easy to find. Selling clean-cut essentials with an elegant and timeless aesthetic, Oxford shirts, merino knits and chinos… this is the place to go for timeless wardrobe staples without breaking the bank.

208 PAUL & FRIENDS

AT: NK DEPARTMENT STORE
Hamngatan 18-20
Norrmalm ①
+46 (0)8 762 83 30
paul-friends.com

On the second floor of the Nordiska Kompaniet luxury department store you'll find the shop-in-shop of Paul & Friends. This multi-brand store opened in 1991 and sells a hand-picked selection of international and Swedish fashion labels. They also stock their own collection, with modern tailored silhouettes for an elegant yet contemporary look.

209 OUR LEGACY

Jakobsbergsgatan 11
Norrmalm ①
+46 (0)8 611 10 10
ourlegacy.se

Swedish menswear brand Our Legacy has been selling trendy quality clothes since it was founded in 2005. They started out with a line of graphic print T-shirts but have since expanded their collection to include footwear and sunglasses. Their menswear collection stands out with its clean lines, simple silhouettes, and neutral colours, creating a sense of effortless sophistication.

210 ASKET

Norrmalmstorg 1
Norrmalm ①
+46 (0)8 28 29 18
asket.com

At Asket they had the ingenious idea of producing basic clothing in a sizing system that goes beyond the standard. Here, all body shapes can snap up timeless pieces that fit perfectly and stand the test of time and temporary trends. With a genuine, modern focus on sustainability, Asket sells one, solid collection, offering full product transparency.

5 essential
FASHION SHOPS
for WOMEN

211 DAGMAR

Smålandsgatan 9
Norrmalm ②
+46 (0)8 20 32 36
houseofdagmar.com

House of Dagmar is a Swedish fashion brand founded by three sisters who decided to follow in the footsteps of their late grandmother. Dagmar was a tailor with a sense of craftsmanship and style. Their feminine and timeless designs are elegantly presented in their graceful store on Smålandsgatan.

212 TOTEME

Biblioteksgatan 5
Norrmalm ①
+46 (0)8 20 38 20
toteme-studio.com

TOTEME was established in New York in 2014 by the Swedish couple Elin Kling and Karl Lindman. Their two-floor store in Stockholm combines upper Manhattan architecture with TOTEME items, as well as hand-picked art books and vintage jewellery.

213 FILIPPA K

Biblioteksgatan 2
Norrmalm ①
+46 (0)8 611 88 03
www.filippa-k.com

Since it was founded in the nineties, Filippa K's mission has been to create a sustainable collection of timeless clothing. The brand continues to be more relevant than ever with its iconic Scandinavian minimalism and their flagship store is a must-visit.

214 RODEBJER

Smålandsgatan 12
Norrmalm ①
+46 (0)8 611 01 17
rodebjer.com

Since the late nineties, designer Carin Rodebjer received numerous awards for her practical, distinctly feminine yet avant-garde silhouettes and modern designs. Rodebjer's flagship store occupies the ground floor of a former bank and has a handsome interior design with clean lines, earthy tones and custom-made elements.

215 ATP ATELIER

Skånegatan 86
Södermalm ⑤
+46 (0)73 962 86 56
atpatelier.com

While on vacation in Italy, two friends got the idea for ATP Atelier. They found a small workshop that produced sandals and realised they could create shoes that combined contemporary Scandinavian design with authentic Italian craftsmanship. Since then, they have released numerous collections of shoes and leather bags.

214 RODEBJER

The 5 best shops for
VINTAGE CLOTHING

---

216 ARKIVET

Nybrogatan 44
Östermalm ②
+46 (0)73 232 70 00
arkivet.com

Arkivet is one of Stockholm's best second-hand shops for trendy items by modern brands. Here they only sell top notch-pieces. The result is a carefully curated collection of handpicked jewellery, bags, clothes, and shoes that is easy to browse.

217 STOCKHOLMS STADSMISSION

Skånegatan 75
Södermalm ⑤
+46 (0)8 684 234 50
stadsmissionen.se

Several charity organisations run great secondhand shops in Stockholm. Next to Nytorget, you'll find one of Stadsmissionen's many shops where you can snap up some bargain clothes. Other places to browse include Myrorna, Humana, Röda Korset and Emmaus.

218 OLD TOUCH

Upplandsgatan 43
Vasastan ⑦
+46 (0)8 34 90 05
oldtouch.se

Around Odenplan in Vasastan you will also find a string of secondhand shops. Old Touch is one of them. The owner, Birgitta Gardner, is inspired by a genuine passion for old things. Browse carefully to find real gems like vintage party dresses, shimmering court shoes, lace veils and a lot of hats.

219 SECOND SUNRISE

Katarina Bangata 69
Södermalm ⑤
+46 (0)8 643 39 15
secondsunrise.se

By now you will probably have realised that Södermalm is the secondhand district. In bustling Katarina Bangata, Second Sunrise sells vintage pieces in a style the owners call 'American workwear filtered through Japan'. Here you can buy high-quality jeans, jackets, shoes and accessories that look better the more you wear them.

220 SIV & ÅKE

Sankt Paulsgatan 20
Södermalm ⑤
+46 (0)76 244 40 06
sivake.se

Sister and brother Anni and Joel Jönsson run Siv & Åke together. This store is full of retro clothes from different eras, which they source from all over the world. Who are Siv & Åke you might wonder? The owner's grandparents, who inspired the shop and its caring, happy aura.

5 of the most interesting
RECORD STORES

221 NOSTALGIPALATSET
Sankt Eriksgatan 101
Vasastan ⑦
+46 (0)8 34 00 61
nostalgipalatset.com

Nostalgipalatset is a treasure trove for vintage record hunters. Their extensive selection of vinyl is stacked in crates, but they also sell movie posters and other memorabilia and collectibles in a basement in Sankt Eriksgatan. Thumbs up for the vinyl player in the store where you can listen to a record before you buy it.

222 BENGANS
Drottninggatan 20
Norrmalm ①
+46 (0)8 723 15 46
bengans.se

Bengans originally opened in Gothenburg in the mid seventies and soon made a name for itself thanks to the low prices and visits of international musicians. Since 2006, Bengans also has a shop in the capital. They sell a wide range of CDs from mainstream artists as well as specific sub genres, vinyl records and movies.

223 FADE RECORDS
Skånegatan 78
Södermalm ⑤
fade.se

A tiny store with an extensive range of new releases and secondhand records, specialising in dance music on vinyl – electro, synth, techno, disco, house and dub. If you're looking for DJ equipment, here's absolutely everything you might possibly need.

224 SNICKARS RECORDS

Hökens gata 11
Södermalm ⑤
+46 (0)73 905 24 22
snickarsrecords.com

Since 1995, DJ Mika Snickars has run Snickars Records next to Mosebacke. They share their space with an art gallery, which you have to walk through before you can get to Snickars. The shop sells secondhand vinyl records focussing on house, hip-hop, soul, funk and jazz. Beside selling records, Snickars also regularly hosts in-store releases and gigs.

225 PET SOUNDS RECORDS

Skånegatan 53
Södermalm ⑤
+46 (0)8 702 97 98
petsounds.se

Pet Sounds has become a popular institution among music lovers. This amazing record store has been ranked one of the top ten in the world, but they have succeeded in remaining a relaxed place where you can find anything from the latest sensations to rare vinyl records. They also host live performances in the shop.

225 PET SOUNDS RECORDS

5 great places for
VINTAGE INTERIOR DESIGN

---

226 STOCKHOLM AUCTIONS

auktionsverket.com
bukowskis.com
metropol.se

In recent years, Stockholm's many auction houses have attracted an increasingly younger audience, lowering the threshold for shopping for vintage items through online bidding. Visit their warehouses to take a closer look at carpets, furniture, mirrors, and decorative items. Either you scan the QR code and bid online, or you can just go to browse for inspiration.

227 VASASTAN VINTAGE WALKS

Vasastan ⑦

Here you can find several small shops and hidden basements that are cluttered with everything from antiques to design objects. Start from Odengatan and walk northwards up Roslagsgatan or Hagagatan, southwards up Upplandsgatan and along Vasaparken.

228 BRANDSTATIONEN

Hornsgatan 64
Södermalm ⑤
+46 (0)8 658 30 10
brandstationenstore.se

Brandstationen is where people who love old and beautiful, but stylish and trendy things shop. Furniture, accessories, plants and lamps… Their selection is inspired by nostalgia. Step inside to discover a range of unusual objects, such as porcelain animals and kitschy neon lights.

229 MODERNITY

Sibyllegatan 6
Östermalm ②
+46 (0)8 20 80 25
modernity.se

Östermalm-based gallery Modernity specialises in the collection and sale of rare and top-of-the-line antiques by the most renowned Scandinavian 20th-century designers. Expect a lot of eye candy and unique collections from post-war designers such as Finn Juhl, Arne Jacobsen and Alvar Aalto.

230 SVENSKA ARMATURER

Svandammsvägen 8
Midsommar-
kransen ④
+46 (0)70 511 01 64
svenskaarmaturer.com

Svenska Armaturer is a wonderland of vintage lamps. The owner, Erik Heggestad, collects and sells lamps, especially mouth-blown glass lamps from the 'Kingdom of Crystal' in the province of Småland but also Italian retro-lamps from the fifties. This store also uses the original moulds to develop new replicas of classic lamp designs.

228 BRANDSTATIONEN

The 5 best shops for
SCANDINAVIAN
INTERIOR DESIGN

———

231 ASPLUND

Sibyllegatan 31
Östermalm ②
+46 (0)8 665 73 60
asplund.org

This interior store has put Scandinavian design on the map with its own collections and hand-picked selection. Thanks to its stylish design language and recurring collaboration with some of Sweden's largest designers, this store is a must for anyone who loves contemporary Nordic design.

232 SVENSKT TENN

Strandvägen 5
Östermalm ②
+46 (0)8 670 16 00
svenskttenn.com

Svenskt Tenn's store is not much of a secret, given its shoreline boulevard location and iconic range. It's more of a must-visit actually. The shop sells an elegant mix of Josef Frank's bold-patterned fabrics and furniture as well as objects by contemporary designers. Tip: visit the cafe, which serves artisanal dishes in a wonderful setting.

233 NORDISKA GALLERIET 1912

Nybrogatan 11
Östermalm ②
+46 (0)8 442 83 60
nordiskagalleriet.se

In 1912, Nordiska Galleriet opened in Nybrogatan in a newly built house in a romantic style. Ever since, this store has become one of Europe's leading shops for exclusive, contemporary design with a comprehensive selection of classic furniture as well as up-and-coming design icons and lighting, accessories and gift items.

234 MALMSTENSBUTIKEN

Humlegårdsgatan 13
Östermalm ②
+46 (0)8 23 33 80
malmsten.se

Here you will find iconic furniture designed by Carl Malmsten, one of the most famous designers of the Swedish Grace movement. Your one-stop-shop for the Giant Toad armchair, the beautiful luminaire of plant decorated screens as well as newly launched Malmsten furniture and beautiful interior design details for your home.

235 NORRGAVEL

Birger Jarlsgatan 27
Norrmalm ①
+46 (0)8 545 220 50
norrgavel.se

Norrgavel is a Swedish company that sells environment-friendly furniture and Scandinavian tableware, textiles, lamps, rugs, and homeware. The company was founded in 1993 out of a desire for furniture that blends in with nature. Ever since then, their contemporary collections have stood the test of time and their sustainable philosophy is more relevant than ever.

5 of the best
BOOKSHOPS

---

236 SÖDERBOKHANDELN HANSSON & BRUCE

Götgatan 37
Södermalm ⑤
+46 (0)8 640 54 32
soderbokhandeln.se

Located in Götgatan since 1927, this is one of Stockholm's oldest bookshops. Step back in time to La belle époque, with books from floor to ceiling, ladders along the walls, comfortable armchairs, relaxed music and a warm atmosphere. Here you'll find genres such as philosophy, history and a great selection of fiction.

236 SÖDERBOKHANDELN HANSSON & BRUCE

237 HEDENGRENS BOKHANDEL
AT: STUREGALLERIAN
Grev Turegatan 13
Östermalm ①
+46 (0)8 611 51 28
hedengrens.se

Hedengrens has a long tradition of guiding customers around the world of literature. Since 1897, books have been sold at this upmarket shop in Östermalm. They have an excellent foreign language section and a strong English section.

238 ADLIBRIS
Kungsgatan 15
Norrmalm ①
adlibris.com

Looking for popular bestsellers, Penguin classics, or cookbooks? Adlibris has exactly what you need. Their wide range of books is organised by category on two floors, and the store also offers a generous selection of yarn and crafts downstairs. Tip: check their calendar for book signings and author talks.

239 PAPERCUT
Krukmakargatan
24-26
Södermalm ⑤
+46 (0)8 13 35 74
papercutshop.se

Papercut is difficult to classify as they carry such a wide range. Books, international and Swedish magazines, films, music, stationery… the list goes on. The collection is carefully selected by the shop's owners, Andreas Fryklund and Alexander Dahlberg, who, separately, ran an independent bookshop and a magazine store before they opened Papercut in 2008.

240 RÖNNELLS ANTIKVARIAT
Birger Jarlsgatan 32
Östermalm ①
+46 (0)8 545 015 60
ronnells.se

It is easy to get lost while browsing Rönnells's endless shelves of oddities and rarities. Scandinavia's largest antiquarian bookshop can be found behind the arched storefront, which dates from 1929. The store has a wide range of books and an excellent English section. Tip: do not miss their popular events.

5 NICHE BOOKSHOPS
you can't afford to miss

241 KONST/IG BOOKS

Åsögatan 124
Södermalm ⑤
+46 (0)8 20 45 20
konstigbooks.com

This independent bookshop is run by Charlotte Ekbom and Helene Boström and is Scandinavia's leading art literature shop. Konst/ig opened in 1994, selling a wide selection of photography, fashion, architecture and graphic design books. Don't forget to check out the magazines, notebooks and prints on the tables.

242 THE ENGLISH BOOKSHOP

Södermannagatan 22
Södermalm ⑤
+46 (0)8 790 55 10
bookshop.se

Even though many bookshops in Stockholm offer an English selection, this place is the only store which really caters to an international audience. In this cosy shop, the shelves are filled with genres ranging from biographies to teenage fiction. They also host talks with authors, with themes such as Nordic Noir.

243 GAMLA STANS BOKHANDEL

Stora Nygatan 7
Gamla stan ③
+46 (0)70 734 51 65
gamlastans
bokhandel.se

Walk down cobbled Stora Nygatan, where you'll find a goldmine for book lovers. Volante publishing company runs this bookshop, stocking a very personal selection of narrative non-fiction, classics, and contemporary bestsellers that make the world wiser and more fun.

244 BOKSLUKAREN

Mariatorget 2
Södermalm ⑤
+46 (0)8 644 21 06
bokslukaren.com

A bookshop for young(er) family members and a great place to escape on a rainy Saturday afternoon. Listen to stories, browse the children's books, and tuck into a mini pastry in the cafe where all the cookies are named after famous characters. How about a Willy Wonka chocolate cupcake or Moominmamma's cake?

245 COMICS HEAVEN

Stora Nygatan 23
Gamla stan ③
+46 (0)8 20 25 16
comicsheaven.se

Whatever comic book title you are looking for, Comics Heaven probably stocks it. Here they sell comics in both Swedish and English, superheroes, merchandise, Marvel, manga, DC and Swedish series such as 91:an. They also have a section of vintage comics, mainly from the eighties onwards.

5 useful shops for
SUSTAINABLE PRODUCTS

246 SVENSK HEMSLÖJD

Norrlandsgatan 20
Norrmalm ①
+46 (0)8 23 21 15
svenskhemslojd.com

As trendy Swedes embrace environmental awareness, they are rediscovering personal handicrafts and high-quality decorative arts with superb workmanship. Svensk Hemslöjd offers a selection of traditional Swedish craftsmanship that is functional, timeless and only becomes more beautiful over time. A great place for good quality souvenirs to take home.

247 GRANIT

Götgatan 31
Södermalm ⑤
+46 (0)72 079 10 13
granit.com

The first Granit store opened its doors in the late nineties. Their motto remains unchanged, i.e., to sell products that simplify life, giving you more time to enjoy it. Here you can find smart storage solutions, kitchen utensils (in other materials than plastic) and interior design that combines aesthetics and function.

248 BYGGFABRIKEN

Högbergsgatan 29
Södermalm ⑤
+46 (0)8 640 25 75
byggfabriken.com

Traditional hinges, switches in bakelite, retro enamel kitchenware… Byggfabriken has everything you might need for your building project. Even though you are not renovating anything at the moment, this shop is worth a visit. You can always find a pretty soap or an interesting book.

249 IRIS HANTVERK

Kungsgatan 55
Norrmalm ①
+46 (0)8 21 47 26
irishantverk.se

After visiting Iris Hantverk, you will not want to use anything else than these Swedish handmade brushes. Since 1870, this small manufacturer has specialised in the craft of producing different types of brushes. Besides their own brush range and kitchen textiles, this shop also sells products for baking, cooking, cleaning and decorating.

250 NATURKOMPANIET

Kungsgatan 4-A
Norrmalm ①
+46 (0)8 723 15 81
naturkompaniet.se

At Naturkompaniet, outdoor life and environmental issues have been a priority from the start. As early as the 1990s, the company sold everything from organic coffee to fleece sweaters made from recycled PET. It's where you go to shop for high-quality equipment for outdoor adventures or everyday life.

5 must-go shops for
HANDMADE CERAMICS

---

251 ERIKA PETERSDOTTER

Sankt Paulsgatan 11
Södermalm ⑤
+46 (0)72 210 92 22
erika-petersdotter.se

Erika Petersdotter's studio and shop is located on Sankt Paulsgatan at Söder. All the ceramics are available in limited quantities and the cups, pots, and candlesticks stand out because of their minimalism, natural colours, Scandinavian simplicity, and Japanese influences.

252 BLÅS & KNÅDA

Hornsgatan 26
Södermalm ⑤
+46 (0)8 642 77 67
blasknada.com

Blås & Knåda is an arts and crafts collective with a gallery and shop. The collective was founded in 1975 when a group of young ceramists and glass artists decided to open a shared sales room. Today, the shelves are lined with unique, playful objects by artisans that span several generations.

253 THE ODE TO

Odengatan 84
Vasastan ⑦
theodeto.com

The Ode To is an online art gallery with a curated selection of one-of-a-kind, contemporary pieces by talented artists and strives to provide a creative platform for women. In their Stockholm showroom next to Vasaparken, you can take a closer look at the sculptures, vases, candleholders, and decorative ceramics. Tip: check the website for the showroom's opening hours.

254 MANOS

Renstiernas gata 22
Södermalm ⑤
+46 (0)73 554 85 25
manos.se

Manos is a shop and workshop that sells ceramics and items in other natural materials such as wood, linen, and mouth-blown glass. The ceramists who run the store create everything themselves, emphasising the beauty of handmade products. They also offer courses at Manos.

255 GUSTAVSBERGS PORSLINSFABRIK

Odelbergs väg 1-C
Gustavsberg
+46 (0)8 570 369 00
gustavsbergs
porslinsfabrik.se

Gustavsberg, to the east of Stockholm, has become a destination for porcelain and ceramics. The Gustavsberg factory has been producing porcelain here since the 19th century, but in recent years, various factory shops were opened here, as well as a porcelain museum. Don't miss G-studio, an association of artisans which is based in the old factory premises, and which organises an 'Open Studio' twice a year that attracts hundreds of visitors.

STADSBIBLIOTEKET

25 NOTABLE BUILDINGS

5

MAJESTIC BUILDINGS

256 RIDDARHUSET

Riddarhustorget 10
Gamla stan ③
+46 (0)8 723 39 90
riddarhuset.se

The House of Nobility was designed by
French-born architect Simon de la Vallée
and is considered one of the most elegant
examples of 17th-century architecture in
Northern Europe. The walls in the Session
Hall are decorated with the coats of arms
of the Swedish aristocracy. Visit the
palace at lunchtime on weekdays or book
a guided tour.

257 NORDISKA MUSEET

Djurgårdsvägen 6-16
Djurgården ⑥
+46 (0)8 519 546 00
nordiskamuseet.se

The Nordic Museum is dedicated to
Sweden's cultural history and ethnography, from the early modern period
to the present-day. Behind the brick and
granite façade of this magnificent building
from 1888, you can learn more about
how the Northerners lived in the past
and about what shaped contemporary
Scandinavian culture.

258 RIKSDAGSHUSET

Riksgatan 3
Gamla stan ③
+46 (0)20 349 000
riksdagen.se

Make sure to walk by Sweden's house of parliament during the golden hour. Seeing the neoclassical building with its Baroque Revival elements against an apricot-pink sky is truly an amazing sight. Tip: There are about 4000 artworks inside Riksdagen. Find out more about the collection during the special art tours.

259 CENTRALPOSTEN

Mäster
Samuelsgatan 70
Norrmalm ①

Have you spotted the prominent art nouveau building in the bustling neighbourhood around Stockholm's Central Station? The Central Post Office building was inaugurated in 1903 and designed by Ferdinand Boberg, one of the most productive architects around the turn of the 20th century. Take a look at the richly sculpted entrance with the pine festoons and small animals.

260 KUNGSTORNEN

Kungsgatan 33
Norrmalm ①

When the neoclassical King's Towers were built in the early twenties, they were the first modern skyscrapers in Europe. The architects, Sven Wallander and Ivar Callmander, were inspired by American buildings, particularly the architecture of Lower Manhattan at the time. Even though you cannot visit the interior, the towers are an eye-catcher in Kungsgatan.

5 iconic
CONTEMPORARY BUILDINGS

---

261 AULA MEDICA

AT: KAROLINSKA INSTITUTET
Nobels väg 6
Solna ⑨

Gert Wingårdh is the famous architect who created Aula Medica, the Karolinska Institutet's lecture hall complex. The architectural landmark is situated on the border between the city and Solna. The building's slightly curved façade with a surface layer consisting of various coloured triangular glass elements is one of the building's stand-out design features.

264 SVEN-HARRY'S KONSTMUSEUM

262 ARKITEKTURSKOLAN

Osquars backe 9
Östermalm ②

The School of Architecture has received several awards over the years. Tham & Videgård designed the ovoid building's exterior in glass and a deep red Corten steel in a nod to the dark red brick façades of the surrounding, older buildings on the KTH Campus.

263 STOCKHOLM WATERFRONT

Nils Ericsons plan 4
Norrmalm ①
*stockholm
waterfront.com*

Distinctive contemporary architecture tends to stir up emotions. But most people agree that White Arkitekter did an excellent job creating this energy-efficient building with an iconic, asymmetric, stainless steel façade.

264 SVEN-HARRY'S KONSTMUSEUM

Eastmansvägen 10-12
Vasastan ⑦
+46 (0)8 511 600 60
sven-harrys.se

How can you overlook this five-floor building, clad in a gold-tinted copper-aluminium-zinc alloy? Nicknamed Guldhuset or 'The Golden House', this spectacular, square building houses an art gallery, a museum and a restaurant, among other things. It was designed by Gert Wingårdh and Anna Höglund of Wingårdh Architects.

265 STRÖMKAJEN'S FERRY TERMINAL BUILDINGS

Strömkajen
Norrmalm ②

When Marge Arkitekter received the commission to build the ferry terminal buildings at Strömkajen, they had to take due account of the site's central location. They created three cone-shaped, sculptural buildings in burnished tombak, that do not detract the attention from the nearby landmarks.

5 must-see
BUILDINGS FROM THE 20TH CENTURY

266 **STOCKHOLM CITY HALL**

Hantverkargatan 1
Kungsholmen ⑧
+46 (0)8 508 290 00
stadshuset.stockholm

This is not much of a hidden secret. In fact, it is probably the most famous silhouette in Stockholm, but still, you should really visit Stockholm's City Hall. The beautiful brick building by Ragnar Östberg was completed in 1923 and is one of the country's most prominent examples of National Romanticism in architecture.

267 **STADSBIBLIOTEKET**

Sveavägen 73
Vasastan ⑦
+46 (0)8 508 309 00
biblioteket.stockholm.se

Stockholm's public library, which was founded in 1928, is one of the capital's most spectacular structures. The distinctive exterior with its circular rotunda has become an iconic landmark and a great example of a style called Swedish Grace. Architect Gunnar Asplund, however, also put a lot of effort into the interior, so make sure to step inside.

268 KONSERTHUSET STOCKHOLM

Hötorget 8
Norrmalm ⓘ
+46 (0)8 506 677 88
konserthuset.se

Another architectural masterpiece is Stockholm's Concert Hall. Inaugurated in 1926, this magnificent neoclassical building was designed by Ivar Tengbom for the Royal Stockholm Philharmonic Orchestra and to host the Nobel Prize Award Ceremony. Take a guided tour or visit the foyers, which normally open one hour before concerts begin.

269 AVICII ARENA

Globentorget 2
Johanneshov
+46 (0)77 131 00 00
aviciiarena.se

Commonly referred to as 'Globen' (the globe), this golf ball-like building is the world's largest spherical building and an iconic feature of Stockholm's skyline. Since its inauguration in 1989, it has hosted a variety of sports events and concerts. In 2021, the arena was named Avicii Arena as a tribute to one of the greatest Swedish artists of our time.

270 KULTURHUSET STADSTEATERN

Sergels torg
Norrmalm ⓘ
+46 (0)8 506 202 00
kulturhuset
stadsteatern.se

Envisioned as a space that could accommodate all art forms, this modernist concrete building with its glass façade, facing Stockholm's most famous public square, was designed in 1974 by the radical post-war architect Peter Celsing. It was built at a time when the city's centre was ravaged by demolition as part of an urban renewal project.

5 of the most
REMARKABLE CHURCHES

---

271 ENGELBREKTS-KYRKAN

Östermalmsgatan 20
Östermalm ②
+46 (0)8 406 98 00

On top of a hill in the heart of the quiet neighbourhood of Lärkstaden, you will find one of Stockholm's largest churches. Designed by Lars Israel Wahlman and completed in 1914, it blends Swedish Art Nouveau with the National Romantic style. The church's 32-metre-high nave, makes it the tallest in Scandinavia.

272 SANKT JOHANNES KYRKA

Johannesgatan 21
Norrmalm ①
+46 (0)8 508 886 50

A good example of Gothic Revival Style churches is Saint John's Church. There has been a cemetery in this location since 1651 but the present-day church was only built 200 years later. Architect Carl Möller won a competition with his plans for a cathedral-like brick-church and in 1890 the building was completed and inaugurated.

273 RIDDARHOLMS-KYRKAN

Riddarholmen
Gamla stan ③
+46 (0)8 402 61 00

Built between 1270 and 1300, Riddarholmen Church is the only remaining medieval abbey in the capital. It has been the burial church of the Swedish monarchs and the aristocracy for over 300 years. We suggest taking a guided tour.

274 HEDVIG ELEONORA KYRKA

Storgatan 2
Östermalm ②
+46 (0)8 545 675 70
hedvigeleonora.se

Next to Östermalmstorg, you can find an octagonal baroque church that was consecrated in 1737. The church is open every day and is one of Stockholm's most popular venues for weddings, christenings and funerals. Attend a church service or a concert, light a candle or just stroll around the church at your leisure.

275 MARKUSKYRKAN

Helsingborgsvägen 51
Johanneshov
+46 (0)8 505 815 00

Markuskyrkan inspires architecture-loving Stockholmers and tourists to travel to the suburbs. In 1960, this modern brick church, surrounded by a birch grove, was finally completed after architect Sigurd Lewerentz's ideas. The modern, brutal functionalist masterpiece was awarded the Sahlin Prize in 1962 for the best building in Sweden.

274 HEDVIG ELEONORA KYRKA

5
PALACES
close to the city

---

276 KINA SLOTT
Drottningholm
+46 (0)8 402 62 80
kungahuset.se

In the same grounds as Drottningholms Palace, which is a UNESCO World Heritage site, you will find this hidden gem. In 1753, King Adolf Fredrik surprised Queen Lovisa Ulrika on her birthday with this fairytale-like Chinese Pavilion. Nowadays visitors can enjoy this exotic milieu and its unique European rococo interiors with chinoiserie from May to September.

277 ROSENDALS SLOTT
Rosendalsvägen 49
Djurgården ⑥
+46 (0)8 402 61 30
kungahuset.se

Rosendal Palace at Djurgården was built between 1823 and 1827 as an escape from the formalities of court life in the Royal Palace for King Karl XIV Johan, the first Bernadotte. Nowadays the pastel pink palace is a unique remnant of the European Empire style. The Swedish variant has the same decorative detailing, but simpler shapes and bright colours.

278 KARLBERGS SLOTT

Karlbergs slottsväg 1
Solna ⑧
+46 (0)8 746 10 00
stockholmslans
museum.se

Located just a stone's throw from the city, this neoclassical palace was transformed into the Royal War Academy in 1792 and has remained a military institution ever since. The beautiful park is open to the public. You can get to the palace by walking along Kungsholmen on the south side of Karlbergskanalen or Vasastan.

279 SKOKLOSTERS SLOTT

Skokloster
+46 (0)8 402 30 60
skoklostersslott.se

Skokloster Castle, which is located in a stunning natural setting on a peninsula on Lake Mälaren's shore, is not exactly near the city, but it is still worth the trip. The building is one of the world's greatest baroque castles and a major monument from a period in Sweden's history when Sweden was one of the most powerful countries in Europe.

280 ULRIKSDALS SLOTT

Slottsallén
Solna ⑨
+46 (0)8 402 61 30
ulriksdalsslott.se

A visit to Ulriksdal Palace is a lovely excursion. The palace was built in 1645 but you will find traces from many different eras here as several rulers left their mark on the palace. Join a guided tour, admire the sculptures in Hedvig Eleonora's Orangery, stroll through Queen Kristina's pleasure garden or check out the Palace Theatre.

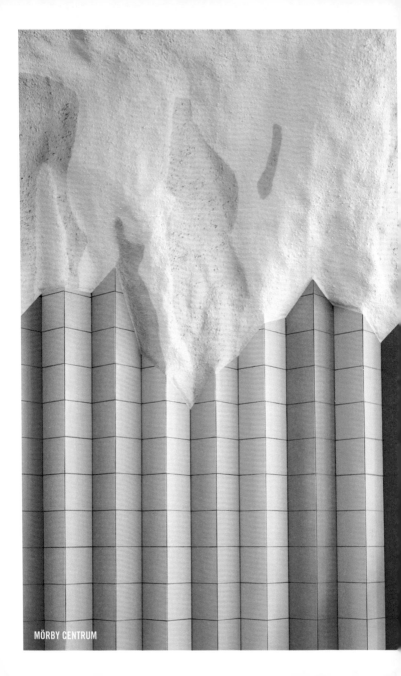
MÖRBY CENTRUM

55 PLACES TO DISCOVER STOCKHOLM

281 MONTELIUSVÄGEN
Södermalm ⑤

This 500-metre-long walking path winds its way up to the top of Mariaberget, offering views across Lake Mälaren, to the City Hall and beyond. The street is named after the historian and archaeologist Oscar Montelius who lived nearby all his life. Enjoy the vista from one of the benches along the way.

282 OBSERVATORIE-LUNDEN
Vasastan ⑦

Located just a few steps away from the vibrant main shopping drag, Observatorie-lunden is the perfect hideaway for a mid-shopping break. The lush park and its old observatory from the 1700s sit on top of a hill, with astonishing views over Vasastan's rooftops and the City Library on its fringe.

283 SKINNARVIKSBERGET
Södermalm ⑤

Skinnarviksberget is a favourite spot with locals. Rising 53 metres above sea level, it is the highest natural viewpoint in town. As you are walking on a mountain surface, suitable shoes are recommended. Come here at sunrise or sunset when the sky turns purple.

284 VÄSTERBRON
Södermalm ④
Kungsholmen ⑧

Inaugurated in 1935, Västerbron became the second stationary link between the southern and northern parts of Stockholm. The bridge has been referenced in Swedish culture in novels, songs and pictures for album covers and music videos and the view over Riddarfjärden makes it a very popular spot for watching the New Year's Eve fireworks.

285 FJÄLLGATAN
Södermalm ⑤

Picturesque Fjällgatan street is surrounded by cute wooden houses from the 1700s on one side and an amazing view over Djurgården, Skeppsholmen, the Old Town and the city's inlet on the other. There are several benches and a cafe to enjoy a coffee break perched on what feels like the top of Stockholm.

285 FJÄLLGATAN

5 remarkable
STATUES

286 JÄRNPOJKE
Trädgårdsgatan 2
Gamla stan ③

Known as the smallest public monument in Sweden, the little iron boy looking at the moon proves that size does not matter. The sculpture is only 15 cm tall and was inaugurated behind the Finnish Church in Old Town in 1967. In wintertime, the statue often wears a knitted hat and scarf.

287 MOLINS FONTÄN
Kungsträdgården
Norrmalm ①

Molin's Fountain is a bronze fountain sculpture in the centre of the Royal Garden, encircled by willows. It was initially made of plaster and exhibited at the Stockholm Exposition of 1866. A bronze version was cast a few years later. The fountain is covered with figures from Nordic mythology.

288 KRISTINA GYLLENSTIERNA
Hantverkargatan /
Ragnar Östbergs plan
Kungsholmen ⑧

Although Stockholm is full of kings on horseback, unfortunately their female counterparts are conspicuously absent. Kristina Gyllenstierna, who defended Stockholm against Denmark in 1520, is an exception to the rule, however. Her statue was the first public statue of a woman in Sweden.

289 MARGARETHA KROOK

Nybrogatan /
Strandvägen
Östermalm ②

On the corner of the Royal Dramatic Theatre you will find the bronze statue of actress Margaretha Krook. Because she didn't like the idea of a cold and unapproachable statue, they heat it to 38° year-round. The monument was placed here in 2002, one year after she passed away. This is where she loved to have a smoke during breaks in the theatre.

290 HEMLÖS RÄV

Drottninggatan /
Strömgatan
Norrmalm ①

It is hard not to pity the poor fox that sits next to the public streams of busy Drottninggatan, just a stone's throw from the country's power centre. The fox is part of the British sculptor Laura Ford's art series Rag and Bone, where animals are placed in the vulnerable situation of homeless people.

290 HEMLÖS RÄV

The 5 most beautiful
UNDERGROUND
STATIONS

---

291 **MÖRBY CENTRUM**
RED LINE
Mörbyleden
Mörby ⑨
sl.se

The Stockholm metro system has been called 'the world's longest art exhibition' with more than 90 stations decorated by over 150 different artists. You can travel in any direction and be amazed at what you see. Mörby Centrum is just one example, where the pastel-painted platform changes to pink, white or grey-green depending on which way you move.

292 **THORILDSPLAN**
GREEN LINE
Kungsholmen ⑧
sl.se

Some metro stations also have art from the 2000s. In 2008, Lars Arrhenius decorated the walls of the outdoor station Thorildsplan in Kungsholmen with tiles in motifs of pixelated symbols from early computer games and icons. He is also the artist behind the Cuckoo clock animation in Stockholm City railway station.

293 ÖSTERMALMSTORG
RED LINE
Östermalm ②
sl.se

Much of the red line was constructed in the sixties, including Östermalmstorg. The artist Siri Derkert was tasked with the transformation of the concrete walls behind the track and the platform walls. She used a special sandblasting technique for her work on women's rights, peace and the environment.

294 HÖTORGET
GREEN LINE
Norrmalm ①
sl.se

On the green line, Hötorget's typical 1950s architecture, signage and iconic light blue tiles were deliberately preserved. In 1998, white neon lights were added along the entire length of the platform, created by the Swedish-Danish artist Gun Gordillo. Hötorget is an excellent example of a typical fifties underground station.

295 KUNGSTRÄDGÅRDEN
BLUE LINE
Arsenalsgatan
Norrmalm ①
sl.se

This station was transformed into an underground garden depicting the history of Kungsträdgården in the seventies, when the unique blue line was built. Cavernous stations like this are not found anywhere else in the world. Tip: join a free guided tour to explore interesting details and learn more about the art in Stockholm's underground.

5
GREEN AREAS
in the city

---

296 BELLEVUEPARKEN
Bellevuevägen 11
Vasastan ⑨

Many tend to head straight for Hagaparken and miss the beautiful Bellevue Park on the southern shore of Brunnsviken. From its highest point you have a panoramic view over the lake. Tip: visit the famous sculptor Carl Eldh's fantastic studio museum in a wooden building from 1919.

297 VITABERGSPARKEN
Borgmästargatan /
Skånegatan
Södermalm ⑤

Vitabergsparken is located on the eastern part of Södermalm. The hilly park has two peaks: on one of them you can find Sofia Kyrka, a beautiful church, and on top of the other is a music pavilion. In summertime, the park is a popular spot for outdoor yoga classes, picnics and open-air theatre.

298 TEGNÉRLUNDEN
Tegnérgatan /
Upplandsgatan
Vasastan ⑦

Boisterous Drottninggatan seems far away in the grove on the hill of Tegnérlunden. The square park was originally built in the late 1800s, but was re-built in 1940. Escape the hustle and bustle with a good book or bring some *fika* from one of the nearby cafes.

299 LILL-JANSKOGEN
Valhallavägen /
Drottning Sofias Väg
Norra Djurgården ⑨

After a 20-minute walk from busy Stureplan, you will reach a wooded area. Lill-Janskogen (Little Jan's forest) at northern Djurgården is a popular forest for recreational activities – you can tell by the joggers, cyclists and walkers. Let Stockholm Olympic Stadium be your starting point and find your way along winding paths among the trees.

300 KRONOBERGSPARKEN
Parkgatan /
Inedalsgatan
Kungsholmen ⑧

If you are spending time in Kungsholmen, it's always good to know that there is a green oasis hidden among the blocks of flats. Planted in the late 19th century on a mountain, this hilly park has grown into a lush space. Here you can find a playground, a Jewish cemetery, ball courts and wild rabbits.

296 BELLEVUEPARKEN

5 great
NEIGHBOURHOODS
to visit

---

301 BIRKASTAN

Metro:
Sankt Eriksplan
Vasastan ⑦

The western part of central Stockholm is home to many restaurants, cafes, small speciality shops, furniture restorers and record stores. The area around Sankt Eriksplan mainly consists of workmen's dwellings built in the Nordic Classicism style in the early 1900s. Tip: drop by Acne's archive shop where you can snap up discounted gems from the past decade.

302 SOFO

Metro:
Medborgarplatsen
Södermalm ⑤

The name SoFo is a pun borrowed from London's and Manhattan's SoHo districts. The Stockholm version is located in Södermalm and short for 'South of Folkungagatan'. This is one of the city's most creative neighbourhoods with innovative retailers and cutting-edge restaurants with a laidback atmosphere.

303 EAST KUNGSHOLMEN

Metro: Rådhuset
Kungsholmen ⑧

The atmosphere in the neighbourhood around Kungsholmstorg is genuinely lovely and quiet, despite being so close to the city. The low-key joie de vivre is very appealing. Head to hidden gem Wijnjas Grosshandel or Fruktaffären to buy some delicacies, or grab a *kanelbulle* from Komet and walk down along the promenade at Norr Mälarstrand to enjoy the incredible views.

304 MIDSOMMAR-KRANSEN & TELEFONPLAN

Metro: Midsommar-kransen
Midsommar-kransen ④

No other suburb offers this much good shopping in one location. Built in the early 20th century to provide housing for the workers of a brick factory and later for the employees of the Ericsson telecom company, this neighbourhood has become an extension of trendy Södermalm. Keep up with all the latest developments on the Kransenkartan Instagram account.

305 GAMLA ENSKEDE

Metro: Sandsborg
Suburbs

The streets in this idyllic suburb to the south of the city were built in the early 1900s to look like a 'typical English' garden city. Stroll past the beautiful houses, eat lunch at the superb, yet intimate, restaurant Matateljén, buy a *fika* bun from the bakery and go on a treasure hunt in the antique shops.

5 must-visit
MARKETS

---

306 HÖTORGET FLEA MARKET
Hötorget
Norrmalm ①

If you're passing through Hötorget on a Sunday, the vegetable and flower stalls will be replaced by flea market vendors and treasure hunters. This cobbled square has been a market place since the 17th century and every Sunday since the mid-1990s, you can browse the tables filled with books, kitchenware, gadgets and pottery.

307 LOPPMARKNADEN VÅRBERG
Fjärdholmsgränd 4
Vårberg
+46 (0)8 710 00 60
loppmarknaden.se

Roll up your sleeves and get ready for some real flea market shopping. One of the capital's oldest and most popular markets is just a 25-minute drive south of Stockholm and is open every day. Expect everything from furniture to glassware, crockery, clocks and clothes at bargain prices.

308 HORNSTULLS MARKNAD
Hornstulls strand 4
Södermalm ④
+46 (0)76 329 15 95
hornstullsmarknad.se

On weekends from April to September, Stockholmers like to flock to the outdoor street market that runs along the lakeside of Årstaviken, which has a fun mix of flea market stalls, antiques, design and art. Tip: arrive with an empty stomach so you can eat your way through the food trucks.

309 BONDENS EGEN MARKNAD

Katarina Bangata
Södermalm ⑤
+46 (0)21 61 090
bondensegen.com

Stockholm has a popular farmer's market, which you can find in Södermalm every Saturday from August to October and on occasional weekends throughout the year. Stroll around the stalls and look, smell and taste before you stock up on organic and locally produced vegetables, cheese, honey, smoked fish and jam. They have another location in Östermalm

310 SKANSENS MARKNADER

AT: BOLLNÄSTORGET
Djurgårds-
slätten 49-51
Djurgården ⑥
+46 (0)8 442 80 00
skansen.se

Skansen is an open-air museum and the perfect place to discover the old Swedish market traditions. On special holidays like Christmas and Easter the charming Böllnas square is filled with food, handicraft, treats and decorations. The locally sourced products are of high quality and are often sold by vendors in old-fashioned clothes.

308 HÖRNSTULLS MARKNAD

5 places where you should
LOOK UP

---

311 **BRUNO LILJEFORS'**
STUDIO
AT: SPORTPALATSET
Sankt
Eriksbron 58-60
Vasastan ⑦

Look up when you walk across Sankt Eriksbron towards Kungsholmen. The famous wildlife painter Bruno Liljefors lived in the top floor apartment of the Sportpalatset. This mint green building, right under the roof lantern, and could often be seen painting on the terrace next to buckets of fish to attract the birds he portrayed.

312 **MILITARY ENSIGN**
OF SWEDEN
AT: KASTELLHOLMEN
Kastellbacken
Södermalm ⑤

When standing at Skeppsholmen, look at the citadel on the island of Kastellholmen. On top of the round tower you will spot the Military Ensign of Sweden, indicating the nation is at peace. If you see the blue-yellow fabric float in the wind, you can rest assured that Sweden is not at war.

313 STOMATOL NEON SIGN
Klevgränd
Södermalm ⑤

In several places in the capital you can still spot neon signs above shops, cafes and cinemas from the last century. One of the most iconic ones is the Stomatol advertisement sign from 1909 that lights up the skyline and has become a prominent local landmark above Slussen.

314 HÖTORGSSKRAPORNA
Sergelgatan
Norrmalm ①

The five 18-storey office buildings you see if you are standing at Sergels torg might not be very impressive nowadays, but they were in the mid-1900s when they were built. Along with the major urban renewal that took place at this time, the five skyscrapers symbolised the hope that Stockholm would become a modern city.

315 SHOEFITI
AT: RÅLIS SKATEPARK
Kungsholmen ⑧

You'll find this concrete skate park, with pipes and bowls for all types of riders in the Rålambshovsparken, just under Lilla Västerbron. Look up and you will see Stockholm's largest collection of shoefiti or shoe tossing. Urban legends seem to have several explanations for what this phenomenon might mean. Regardless, the dangling sneakers add a fun touch to the bridge.

5

FASCINATING CEMETERIES

---

316 ADOLF FREDRIKS KYRKOGÅRD

Holländargatan 16

Norrmalm ①

The Adolf Fredrik Church in the city centre is known for its fine works of art and the graves of many prominent Swedes in its cemetery. Here you can find the graves of Swedish Prime Minister Hjalmar Branting's and that of Prime Minister Olof Palme, who was assassinated in 1986, just a block away from the church.

317 KATARINA KYRKOGÅRD

Högbergsgatan 13

Södermalm ⑤

Saint Catherine's Church in Södermalm was rebuilt twice after being destroyed by fire, the second time was in the 1990s. Several famous Swedes are buried in the cemetery surrounding the church. Many of their graves are located along the main gravel road.

318 NORRA BEGRAVNINGS-PLATSEN

Solna kyrkväg 171

Solna ⑨

One of the country's largest burial grounds is Norra begravningsplatsen in Solna, which dates from the 1900s and is the burial site of several authors, politicians and scientists. When you take a stroll among the graves, you will recognise the names of many Nobel Prize winners, including that of Alfred Nobel himself.

319 SKOGSKYRKOGÅRDEN
Sockenvägen 392
Gamla Enskede

The UNESCO World Heritage Woodland Cemetery is a major cemetery and an architectural masterpiece. The famous architects Gunnar Asplund and Sigurd Lewerentz received the commission to design it in 1915. Its chapels, crematorium and tranquil landscape design reflect the evolution from Nordic Classicism to mature Functionalism.

320 MOSAISKA BEGRAVNINGS-PLATSEN ARONSBERG
Alströmergatan
Kungsholmen ⑧

This Jewish cemetery in Kungsholmen, which is surrounded by apartment buildings, is so well hidden that passers-by and even the locals are sometimes surprised to see it is there. The Mosaic Aronsberg burial site was founded in 1776 and is named after Aaron Isaac, the first Jew who was allowed to settle in Sweden without renouncing his Jewish faith.

319 SKOGSKYRKOGÅRDEN

5 places related to
GRETA GARBO

321 GARBOHUSET
Blekingegatan 32
Södermalm ⑤

The divine Hollywood actress was born as Greta Lovisa Gustafsson in a three-bedroom flat at Blekingegatan 32 in Södermalm in 1905, when the neighbourhood was still a working-class slum. This building has since been demolished and the area has become gentrified, but the house that stands here today is still referred to as the Garbo House.

325 FILMSTADEN

322 GRETA GARBOS TORG
Katarina Bangata 41
Södermalm ⑤

In 1992, the City of Stockholm decided to name the lush cobblestone square at the intersection of Katarina Bangata and Södermannagatan in honour of Greta Garbo. She went to the nearby Katarina Södra school until she was 14 years old. Even as a child, Garbo already dreamt of becoming an actress.

323 DRAMATEN
Nybroplan
Östermalm ②
dramaten.se

In 1922, Greta Garbo was accepted to the Royal Dramatic Theatre's Acting School at the age of 17, as the youngest student in her class. She studied there until she was cast in films, finally leaving the school after two years.

324 PUB
NOW: HAYMARKET
BY SCANDIC HOTEL
Hötorget 13-15
Norrmalm ①

Garbo began her career as a sales clerk selling hats at the fashionable PUB department store around 1920. She was cast in the store's advertisements for women's clothing. One day, when working at PUB, Garbo caught the eye of a famous director who gave her a part in his film, *Peter the Tramp*.

325 FILMSTADEN
Greta Garbos väg 3
Solna ⑨
filmstadenskultur.se

During the early 20th century, Filmstaden was one of the most modern film studios in Europe where more than 400 films were made. In 1924, Greta Garbo played a principal part in *The Saga of Gösta Berling*, which was partly filmed here and which led to a Hollywood contract for Garbo. She is honoured with a statue here.

5 places that are featured in
NORDIC NOIR NOVELS & TV

---

326 STOCKHOLM POLICE HEADQUARTERS

Kungsholms-
gatan 33-47
Kungsholmen ⑧

Stockholm's central police station at Kungsholmen has been referenced in several crime novels and TV series over the years. It is cited most frequently in Arne Dahl's series about the fictional group of Swedish crime investigators, called *A-Gruppen* (the Intercrime Group). The headquarters consist of several buildings built between 1911 and 1972.

327 THE HEIGHTS OF SÖDER

Södermalm ⑤

After the success of Stieg Larsson's *Millennium* trilogy, crime novel fans have started to travel to the sites where the stories unfold. If you want to follow in Mikael Blomkvist and Lisbeth Salander's footsteps, you must visit the historic quarters around Bellmansgatan 1 and Fiskargatan 9 where they live and where several key scenes are set.

328 STUREPLAN

Östermalm ②

Jens Lapidus's thriller *Easy Money* tells the story of a student, who lives a double life driving a taxi illegally and who becomes involved with drug dealers to fund his expensive lifestyle on Stureplan.

329 FRIHAMNEN PORT
Östermalm ②

In a genre where the main characters are often men, it was kind of liberating when Liza Marklund finally introduced the female journalist Annika Bengtzon as the protagonist of her first crime novel in 1998. Frihamnen Port is featured in the third book of this bestselling series, titled *Paradise*, when two bodies are found on the dock.

330 BERGSUNDS STRAND 31
Södermalm ④

During the sixties and seventies, Maj Sjöwall and Per Wahlöö wrote novels about Martin Beck of the special homicide division of the Swedish national police. All of the books have since been turned into TV series and Beck's balcony is a frequent feature. You can find this brick building if you walk along Bergsunds strand in Hornstull.

327 THE HEIGHTS OF SÖDER

5 annual
EVENTS
not to miss

---

331 STOCKHOLM DESIGN WEEK & STOCKHOLM CREATIVE EDITION

stockholm designweek.com

stockholm creativeedition.com

Stockholm Design Week takes place in February. It was first organised in 2002 and since then it has developed into the most important platform for Scandinavian design with the Stockholm Furniture Fair as its main event. Tip: also keep an eye on the upcoming Stockholm Creative Week, an independent design week that takes place in May.

332 KULTURNATT STOCKHOLM

kulturnattstockholm.se

Since 2010, the City of Stockholm has developed a comprehensive programme of cultural events that are open to the public on one special night in April. Art, dance, music, fashion and literature… This is a great opportunity to discover something you are interested in. It's like a *smörgåsbord* of culture.

333 MIDSUMMER

The Midsummer celebrations are possibly the most characteristic festivity in Sweden. Many city dwellers take a break in the archipelago or in the countryside, but there are several celebrations in the city as well. Skansen, Sturehof, Mosebacketerrassen, Fjäderholmarna and Stallmästaregården are just a few examples of where you can join in and celebrate this tradition.

334 STOCKHOLM PRIDE

stockholmpride.org

The pride festival takes place in the middle of summer. Since its first edition in 1998, it has grown into the largest gay pride in Scandinavia. There are events all over the city, but the main venue hosts music acts, shows, workshops and seminars. Tip: the colourful parade is always a fun event.

335 STOCKHOLM FILMFESTIVAL

stockholmfilmfestival.se

Stockholm Filmfestival takes place every year in November, lasting four days. The festival screens films from countries all over the world and hosts events and award ceremonies for professionals in the movie industry. This is a great opportunity to see quality films in some of the town's most charming cinemas.

ARKDES

60 PLACES TO ENJOY CULTURE

———

The 5 best
ART GALLERIES

---

336 ANDRÉHN-SCHIPTJENKO
Linnégatan 31
Östermalm ②
+46 (0)8 612 00 75
andrehn-schiptjenko.com

Since its inception in 1991, Cilène Andréhn and Marina Schiptjenko's gallery has become one of the leading galleries in Scandinavia. They showcase works by contemporary artists in different mediums such as painting, sculpture, photography, film, and performance. The gallery also has a second space in Paris.

337 GALLERI MAGNUS KARLSSON
AT: KONSTAKADEMIEN
Fredsgatan 12
Norrmalm ①
+46 (0)8 660 43 53
gallerimagnus karlsson.com

Galleri Magnus Karlsson is located on the ground floor of The Royal Swedish Academy of Fine Arts. The gallery is considered one of the most interesting galleries in the country since its start in Västerås in 1990. It shows the work of emerging Swedish artists and promotes them internationally.

338 GALERIE NORDENHAKE
Hudiksvallsgatan 8
Vasastan ⑦
+46 (0)8 21 18 92
nordenhake.com

If you visit Stockholm's art street in Vasastan, the so-called Stockholm Gallery District, then you must stop at Galerie Nordenhake. Founded in 1976 in Malmö, it moved to Stockholm in 1986. It is now a leading European art gallery.

339 LOYAL GALLERY

Odengatan 3
Vasastan ⑦
+46 (0)8 680 77 11
loyalgallery.com

Under the direction of Martin Lilja and Amy Giunta, Loyal Gallery is actively involved with the New York and Los Angeles art scenes. The gallery is located in the former Embassy of Brazil in Stockholm's Lärkstaden and is considered an important player, promoting young international artists in Stockholm.

340 GALLERY STEINSLAND BERLINER

Bondegatan 70
Södermalm ⑤
+46 (0)8 740 60 60
steinslandberliner.com

Gallery Steinsland Berliner (GSB) is run by Jeanette Steinsland and Jacob Kampp Berliner and opened its doors in Södermalm in 2008. The gallery attracts a young and art-conscious audience and aims to showcase all art disciplines, from performance to paintings. Expect to find emerging as well as established artists.

340 GALLERY STEINSLAND BERLINER

The 5 best museums for
CONTEMPORARY ART

---

341 **MODERNA MUSEET**
Exercisplan 4
Skeppsholmen ⑥
+46 (0)8 520 235 00
modernamuseet.se

Interested in Stockholm's collection of Dalí, Picasso and Matisse? Head to Skeppsholmen, where Moderna Museet is located. This state museum collects, preserves, exhibits and promotes knowledge about 20th and 21st-century art. In addition to modern classic and contemporary art, this building also has a restaurant and a popular design shop.

342 **MAGASIN III**
Frihamnsgatan 28
Östermalm ②
+46 (0)8 545 680 40
magasin3.com

Magasin III is a contemporary art museum, showcasing works by international established artists. It has become a leading institution for contemporary art in Europe, loaning works to other institutions around the world. The museum, which is located in a former warehouse in Stockholm's free port, provides a platform for influential and engaging art.

343 SVEN-HARRYS KONSTMUSEUM

Eastmansvägen 10
Vasastan ⑦
+46 (0)8 511 600 60
sven-harrys.se

At Sven-Harrys, it's not just the golden exterior that merits your attention. While the exhibitions in this 400-square-metre art museum are definitely worth visiting, the real highlight can be found on the roof: a replica of the former home of its founder Sven Harry. The museum boasts one of Sweden's largest private collections of Nordic art.

344 BONNIERS KONSTHALL

Torsgatan 19
Vasastan ⑦
+46 (0)8 736 42 55
bonnierskonsthall.se

This art institution is located just a few blocks from Vasaparken. The spectacular building with its rounded corners and glass façade was designed by Johan Celsing Arkitektkontor. Since its opening in 2006, Bonniers Konsthall has earned a reputation as leading independent and non-profit institution for Swedish and international contemporary art.

345 LILJEVALCHS KONSTHALL

Djurgårdsvägen 60
Djurgården ⑥
+46 (0)8 508 313 30
liljevalchs.se

When Liljevalchs opened in 1916, it was the country's first independent contemporary art museum. Its mission was to make art more accessible to the public. Its famous juried Spring Salon marks the opening of each new artistic year and is followed by at least four large and lavish exhibitions of art and design.

346 FÄRGFABRIKEN

347 ARTIPELAG

5 places to enjoy
ART IN THE SUBURBS

346 FÄRGFABRIKEN
Lövholmsbrinken 1
Liljeholmen ④
+46 (0)8 645 07 07
fargfabriken.se

This art venue is located in an industrial building from 1889. Fairs, exhibitions, seminars, clubs and workshops are organised behind the brick façade, which is home to a 'laboratory of the contemporary'. From here you can enjoy a lovely view over the water, separating Liljeholmen from the small island of Reimersholme.

347 ARTIPELAG
Artipelagstigen 1
Gustavsberg
+46 (0)8 570 130 00
artipelag.se

The name 'Artipelag' is a combination of Art, Activities and Archipelago. This cultural meeting point, surrounded by pine trees, cliffs and brackish water, is definitely worth a visit. Explore the exhibitions in the art gallery, admire the building's architecture or enjoy the surroundings from the restaurant's outdoor terrace with a great view.

348 MARABOUPARKEN
Löfströms allé 7–9
Sundbyberg
+46 (0)8 29 45 90
marabouparken.se

The Marabouparken art gallery and sculpture park is located in the suburb of Sundbyberg. During the past fifty years, it was a visionary landscaped recreational facility for the employees of the Marabou chocolate factory, but since 2005 the park and the former cocoa laboratory are run by a foundation that exhibits the work of contemporary artists.

349 MILLESGÅRDEN
Herserudsvägen 32
Lidingö
+46 (0)8 446 75 90
millesgarden.se

Many of Stockholm's most famous sculptures were created by artist Carl Milles. Together with his wife, painter Olga Milles, he bought a house on a cliff, high above Lake Värtan in 1906. Their home has since been transformed into a well-known museum popular for its vast sculpture garden and exhibitions.

350 TENSTA KONSTHALL
Taxingegränd 10
Spånga
+46 (0)8 36 07 63
tenstakonsthall.se

Tensta Konsthall's ambition is to be an institution that is also committed to the local community. The gallery is located in the suburb of Tensta and was inaugurated in 1998 thanks to a local grassroots initiative. They still work with international as well as Swedish artists, often in partnership with local organisations.

5 of the best
STATE MUSEUMS

---

351 ARKDES

Exercisplan 4
Skeppsholmen ⑥
+46 (0)8 520 235 00
arkdes.se

ArkDes is the Swedish Centre for Architecture and Design, previously known as the Museum of Architecture. Located next to Moderna Museet, ArkDes hosts a permanent exhibition about architecture in Sweden – perfect for understanding the golden age of Swedish Modernism and its context. ArkDes also organises temporary thematic exhibitions.

352 NATIONALMUSEUM

Södra Blasieholms-
hamnen 2
Norrmalm ②
+46 (0)8 519 543 00
nationalmuseum.se

Nestled in the heart of Stockholm, majestic Nationalmuseum stands as a testament to the rich cultural heritage of Sweden. Its collection spans centuries and encompasses remarkable works of art, including paintings, sculptures, and design. You can spend many hours here so start with a lunch in the exquisite restaurant which has a magnificent view of the royal palace.

353 NATURHISTORISKA RIKSMUSEET

Frescativägen 40
Norra Djurgården ⑨
+46 (0)8 519 540 00
nrm.se

Want to know more about natural history, biology and geology? In this majestic building from 1916 you can see giant animal bones, fossils, sparkling stones from the Earth's core and an IMAX cinema called Cosmonova, which is also the largest planetarium in Sweden.

354 HALLWYLSKA MUSEET

Hamngatan 4
Norrmalm ②
+46 (0)8 402 30 99
hallwylskamuseet.se

The Hallwyl House next to Berzelii Park is a glorious time capsule. The house that belonged to the Von Hallwyls family around 1900 is now a museum. Experience the modernity and eclectic luxuries of the Stockholm of yore as you walk through the beautiful rooms in this palatial residence.

355 MEDELHAVSMUSEET

Fredsgatan 2
Norrmalm ①
+46 (0)10 456 12 00
medelhavsmuseet.se

Sweden's Museum of Mediterranean and Near Eastern Antiquities showcases ancient culture, beauty, treasures and traditions of the Middle East and Greece, Egypt, and the Roman Empire. The Bagdad Cafe upstairs is a hidden gem. Tip: the sister museum, which focuses on ethnography and is located in the lush greenery of Djurgården, is also worth a visit.

The 5 most
UNUSUAL MUSEUMS

356 **VRAK**
Djurgårdsstrand 17
Djurgården ⑥
+46 (0)8 519 549 14
vrak.se

Discover the captivating world of maritime history at Vrak – Museum of Wrecks in Stockholm. Immerse yourself in the stories of sunken ships, archaeological treasures, and the mysteries that lie beneath the waves. Through interactive exhibits and fascinating artefacts, this museum offers a unique window into the hidden depths of Sweden's maritime heritage.

357 **SCENKONSTMUSEET**
Sibyllegatan 2
Östermalm ②
+46 (0)8 519 567 00
scenkonstmuseet.se

The Museum of Performing Art is the result of a merger between the Music Museum, the Theatre Museum, and the Puppet Museum. It houses extensive collections of objects that showcase the rich heritage of these art forms. Visitors of all ages can engage in interactive activities, making it an enriching experience for everyone.

358 LIVRUSTKAMMAREN
AT: KUNGLIGA SLOTTE
Slottsbacken 3
Gamla stan ③
+46 (0)8 402 30 30
livrustkammaren.se

Established in 1628 by King Gustav II Adolph, the Royal Armoury is Sweden's oldest museum. It is situated in the cellars of the Royal Palace in Stockholm and exhibits the ceremonial costumes of Sweden's royals. See the blood and mud-marked uniforms that were worn in wars or the beautiful garments for royal coronations, weddings and funerals.

359 SPRITMUSEUM
Djurgårdsstrand 9
Djurgården ⑥
+46 (0)8 121 313 03
spritmuseum.se

Swedes have a bittersweet relationship with alcohol. They love the excitement but are aware of its drawbacks. The exhibitions at the Museum of Spirits will teach you more about the Swedish drinking culture, but you can also visit the colourful 'The Absolut Art Collection', take part in tastings and visit the splendid restaurant, bar and museum shop.

360 KVINNOHISTORISKA
kvinnohistoriska.se

Stockholm's museum of women's history operates outside the confines of a permanent building. Rather than being tied to a fixed location, this museum takes on various forms throughout the city, offering tours, exhibitions, talks, and an array of activities. Collaborations with established museums shed light on the significant contributions of women.

5

HIDDEN WORKS

at the most visited museums

---

361 PROPPLODSHÅLET
AT: VASAMUSEET
Galärvarvsvägen 14
Djurgården ⑥
+46 (0)8 519 548 80
vasamuseet.se

Ironically, one of the greatest points of interest on the warship Vasa was a tiny hole, only 1 cm in diameter. Thousands of visitors tend to miss this little detail, marked with a red ring on the upper deck. This hole is where Anders Franzén's coring device hit the ship when he discovered the wreck of the Vasa in 1956.

362 ROSLIN'S SELF-PORTRAIT WITH HIS WIFE MARIE SUZANNE GIROUST
AT: NATIONALMUSEUM
Södra Blasieholms-hamnen 2
Norrmalm ②
+46 (0)8 519 543 00
nationalmuseum.se

Most people associate Sweden's National Museum with the painting *The Lady with the Veil* by Alexander Roslin. But what people don't know is that there is another work here, which Roslin painted together with his wife. In this self-portrait, she is depicted as an artist, painting a portrait of Henrik Wilhelm Peill in 1767. It is a multi-faceted painting that was part of a private collection for many years.

363 KRONBERGS ATELJÉ
AT: SKANSEN
Djurgårds-
slätten 49-51
Djurgården ⑥
+46 (0)8 442 80 00
skansen.se

A common misconception is that the open-air museum and zoo Skansen is all about animals, but the buildings here are just as intriguing. A yellow house from 1912 is particularly interesting. This was the famous painter Julius Kronberg's studio, where the pop group ABBA shot the cover for their last album, *Visitors*, in 1981.

364 MONUMENT TO THE LAST CIGARETTE
AT: MODERNA MUSEET
Exercisplan 4
Skeppsholmen ⑥
+46 (0)8 520 235 00
modernamuseet.se

If you visit Moderna Museet, don't forget to look at Erik Dietman's concrete sculpture in the museum garden. As an artist, Dietman was intelligent but he also had an excellent sense of humour, taking a critical approach to art. Curious what you'll see once you climb up the ladder of this pompous monument?

365 BALKÅKRA RITUAL OBJECT
AT: HISTORISKA MUSEET
Narvavägen 13-17
Östermalm ②
+46 (0)8 519 556 00
historiska.se

One of the most remarkable ancient archaeological treasures in Sweden is the so-called Balkåkra Ritual Object at the Swedish History Museum, but many visitors tend to miss it. It's a shame, because this mysterious object is 3500 years (!) old and its use and purpose remain unknown.

364 MONUMENT TO THE LAST CIGARETTE

The 5 best places to
WATCH A MOVIE

---

366 **INDIO CINEMA**
Hornstulls strand 3
Södermalm ④
+46 (0)8 669 95 00
cinema.indio.se

Indio Cinema is one of Stockholm's few remaining single-screen cinemas from the 1940s. Here they screen a curated selection of films and host Q&As and performances. This independent arthouse cinema also runs the restaurant next door, which serves Japanese food with Peruvian influences.

367 **ZITA FOLKETS BIO**
Birger Jarlsgatan 37
Norrmalm ①
+46 (0)8 23 20 20
zita.se

Inaugurated in 1913, this is Stockholm's oldest movie theatre. The repertoire includes arthouse films (always screened in their original language) that are hard to find in the big cinemas, short movies, documentaries, silent films and festivals dedicated to specific countries or regions.

368 **SOMMARBIO**
AT: RÅLAMBSHOVSPARKEN
Kungsholmen ⑧
stockholmfilmfestival.se

For a couple of days in August, people gather on the lawn in Rålambshovs-parken for a film night. The Stockholm International Film Festival organises this annual event, which has become a real tradition among the locals. Bring your friends, a blanket and a picnic and watch some classic films on the outdoor screen.

369 GRAND

Sveavägen 45
Norrmalm ⓘ
+46 (0)8 562 600 00
filmstaden.se

In the early thirties, architect Björn Hedvall (who considered himself somewhat of a cinema specialist) was tasked with transforming this former church into a cinema. Nowadays, the theatre has four auditoriums and it has undergone renovations over the years, but the intarsia (a technique of woodworking) doors with pictures of iconic film stars are original.

370 BIO CAPITOL

Sankt Eriksgatan 82
Vasastan ⑦
+46 (0)8 511 657 81
capitolbio.se

Thanks to a crowdfunding campaign, a group of movie fans brought one of Stockholm's most beautiful cinemas back to life. Capitol was built in 1926 and many of its original art deco-vibe details have been maintained. This independent two-screen cinema also serves snacks which you can bring into the cinema.

367 ZITA FOLKETS BIO

The 5 best
THEATRES

---

371 ROYAL DRAMATIC THEATRE

Nybroplan
Östermalm ②
+46 (0)8 667 06 80
dramaten.se

If you want to see Sweden's top acting talents in action, then head to the beautiful, golden building that locals call 'Dramaten'. This is where the careers of stars such as Ingrid Bergman and Greta Garbo started. Ingmar Bergman considered the Royal Dramatic Theatre his second home.

372 OSCARSTEATERN

Kungsgatan 63
Norrmalm ①
+46 (0)8 20 50 00
oscarsteatern.se

Stockholm's best-known musical theatre is located behind a majestic Jugendstil façade on Kungsgatan. The Oscar Theatre was built in 1906 and over the years has become the place to go for glitz and glamour. Many of its productions are adapted from English-speaking musicals, so even a foreign audience will recognise melodies from Broadway and the West End.

373 KULTURHUSET STADSTEATERN

Sergels torg
Norrmalm ①
+46 (0)8 506 202 12
kulturhuset
stadsteatern.se

Kulturhuset Stadsteatern is a publicly funded institution and Sweden's most popular theatre. The theatre wing was built in 1960 and is the largest of its kind in Northern Europe. With a variety of cultural events, popular performances and a very busy programme, we recommend booking well ahead.

374 ORIONTEATERN

Katarina Bangata 77
Södermalm ⑤
+46 (0)8 643 88 80
orionteatern.se

The Orion Theatre in Södermalm is Sweden's largest avant-garde theatre and has been staging experimental works since 1983. In a huge, former mechanical workshop they offer an innovative cultural experience that challenges and inspires visitors. They also collaborate with companies from around the world.

375 STRINDBERGS INTIMA TEATER

Barnhusgatan 20
Norrmalm ①
+46 (0)8 545 110 44
strindbergs
intimateater.se

Sweden's most famous playwright, August Strindberg has a theatre that is dedicated to him and his plays. Strindbergs Intima Teater at Norra Bantorget square was founded in 1907 and managed by Strindberg himself together with actor August Falck. The repertoire and most performances are still by or about Strindberg.

5 great venues for
LIVE MUSIC

---

376 FASCHING
Kungsgatan 63
Norrmalm ①
+46 (0)8 20 00 66
fasching.se

Since its opening in 1977, Fasching has become Scandinavia's most famous jazz concert venue thanks to the live music and electric atmosphere. In addition to its legendary jazz clubs and live performances by Swedish and international talent, they also host soul, funk, disco, and Latino music nights.

377 KAIJA'S
Storgatan 44
Östermalm ②
+46 (0)73 423 35 04
kaijasalong.com

Nestled in the capital's most elegant quarters, Sweden's tiniest live stage is a vibrant music venue where emerging artists and local bands take to the stage. With its intimate atmosphere, diverse line-up, and cosy bar, this hidden secret is a great place to enjoy an authentic experience.

378 DEBASER STRAND

Hornstulls strand 4
Södermalm ④
+46 (0)8 658 63 50
debaser.se

Debaser Strand is tucked away below the waterfront of Hornstulls strand. This is a popular concert and club venue with Stockholm's music lovers. With a fully booked schedule and a varied line-up, this is the place to go for a concert or to go dancing almost every day of the week.

379 MUSIKALISKA

Nybrokajen 11
Norrmalm ①
+46 (0)8 407 17 00
musikaliskakvarteret.se

The concerts at Musikaliska are known for their high artistic quality and the venue's acoustically rich environment, enhancing the listening experience for the audience. Sweden's first concert hall, this place opened in 1877. Today it is a cluster of stages, restaurants, bars and in the summer, their courtyard is a popular hang-out for clubbers.

380 NALEN

Regeringsgatan 74
Norrmalm ①
+46 (0)8 505 292 00
nalen.com

Nalen, a beautifully restored historic building in central Stockholm, is a multi-faceted venue for live music, club nights, and a lively bar. With a focus on jazz, soul, and world music, its multiple stages and welcoming ambience attract a wide range of music enthusiasts, perfect for discovering new sounds while enjoying a drink.

The 5 best
MUSIC FESTIVALS

---

381 ROSENDAL GARDEN PARTY
Valmundsvägen
Djurgården ⑥
rosendal.com

Nestled amidst lush greenery in Djurgården, this enchanting four-day event offers a vibrant blend of music and food. Enjoy live performances by headliners in the company of other well-chosen stars and timeless favourites and bask in the joyous atmosphere of this unforgettable garden party experience.

382 DEPARTMENT
UNDER: VÄSTERBRON BRIDGE
Långholmen ④
departmentfestival.com

Department, an electronic music festival, takes place at Långholmen, an idyllic yet accessible location. With an eclectic line-up that caters to techno and house fans, this eagerly anticipated event lights up the dancefloor. In addition to exceptional music, this festival also rolls out innovative initiatives to minimise its environmental footprint.

383 STOCKHOLM CULTURE FESTIVAL
VARIOUS LOCATIONS
kulturfestivalen. stockholm.se

During five bustling summer days every year, Stockholm Culture Festival fills streets and squares in downtown Stockholm with all kinds of (free!) cultural events. Its comprehensive programme includes everything from pop and rock performances to workshops, theatre and much more.

384 LOLLAPALOOZA
AT: GÄRDET
Östermalm ②
lollastockholm.com

The Lollapalooza music festival attracts large audiences thanks to international superstars and some of Sweden's best artists. Performances usually include a wide range of genres and the festival has always been a platform for non-profit and political groups and many visual artists.

385 STOCKHOLM JAZZ FESTIVAL
ALL OVER STOCKHOLM
stockholmjazz.se

Every autumn, one of Sweden's oldest festivals has people flocking to venues all over Stockholm over a ten-day period, from smaller jazz bars to the city's largest concert halls. Stockholm Jazz Festival was established in 1980 and is considered one of Europe's most pleasant music festivals.

The 5 best
OUTDOOR CLUBS

---

386 **F12**
  Fredsgatan 12
  Norrmalm ①
  f12sthlm.se

If you walk past the grand staircase of the historic building that houses the Royal Swedish Academy of Fine Arts at night, you might notice neon lights, some heavy beats and a crowd. This iconic terrace club is a summer-only spot with a spectacular view over the Old Town and Riddarholmen.

387 **HÄKTET**
  Hornsgatan 82
  Södermalm ④
  +46 (0)8 84 59 10
  haktet.se

Häktet may not tick all the boxes of a club, but their courtyard is too good not to mention. During the rest of the year, Häktet is a top-notch bar, delicious restaurant, where they also host music quizzes and live performances, and in the summer, they open up their courtyard.

388 TRÄDGÅRDEN

Hammarby Slussväg 2
Södermalm ⑤
+46 (0)8 644 20 23
tradgarden.com

Not mentioning Trädgården, Stockholm's premier outdoor club, would be a massive mistake. As the ultimate summertime destination under Skanstull Bridge, this iconic establishment boasts multiple dance floors, bars, live performances, and leisure areas for socialising. Tip: Check out Vingården, a colourful area designed by shooting star Gustaf Westman.

389 TERRASSEN & KVARTERET

AT: SLAKTHUSEN
Slakthusgatan 6
Johanneshov
slakthusen.se

An old slaughterhouse in Stockholm's meatpacking district serves as a vibrant nightclub area. The industrial setting provides a backdrop for immersive club experiences, featuring diverse music genres and several dance floors. During the warmer months, they open up their 600-square-metre rooftop, Terrassen, and an outdoor area called Kvarteret.

390 STADSGÅRDS-TERMINALEN

AT: STADSGÅRDEN
Södermalm ④
stadsgards
terminalen.com

In the middle of Slussen's construction chaos, you'll find a lively cultural centre that always has a surprise in store. The converted boat terminal houses several stages for both clubbing and live music performances and is open year-round. In the summer, the terrace overlooking Stockholm's inlet is fully booked with DJ gigs.

5 great places to join Stockholm's
NIGHTLIFE

---

391 SÖDRA TEATERN

Mosebacke torg 1-3
Södermalm ⑤
sodrateatern.com

Stockholm's oldest theatre offers an eclectic programme and a diverse line-up of DJs and live performances, for an immersive clubbing experience. The venue has multiple dance floors, bars, and a unique atmosphere, attracting a lively crowd looking to enjoy an unforgettable night of music, dancing, and entertainment.

392 SPY BAR

Birger Jarlsgatan 20
Östermalm ①
stureplansgruppen.se/
nightlife/spy-bar

Spy Bar, a renowned establishment in a Renaissance style building at Stureplan, attracts a diverse clientele ranging from media personalities, celebrities and club kids. Arrive early as the queue can be quite long. Once inside, Spy Bar offers an exhilarating nightlife experience.

393 SLAKTHUSET

Slakthusgatan 6
Johanneshov
slakthusen.se

Slakthuset is a well-known nightclub and events venue, located to the south of Stockholm. Against an industrial backdrop with multiple dance floors, bars, and stages, Slakthuset hosts a variety of music events, including EDM parties, live performances, and themed club nights, attracting a diverse crowd of night owls.

394 UNDER BRON

Hammarby Slussväg 2
Södermalm ⑤
+46 (0)8 644 20 23
underbron.com

No, the world doesn't end when extremely popular Trädgården closes for the season in September. During autumn and winter, Under Bron (an indoor club in the same location) takes over. The walls are decorated with works by different artists, the music is electronic, the vibe 'underground' and, what's more, here you can dance the night away until 5 am.

395 NATTEN

AT: B-K
Frihamnsgatan 14
Frihamnen

Instead of a permanent nightclub, Natten is an event that occurs every once in a while. It's hosted in an iconic warehouse building which the locals call *Banankompaniet,* and which has been transformed into a club venue. Natten is extremely popular and best described as teen disco for adults. Power ballads, cheek-to-cheek dancing, singalongs… What's not to love?

TEKNISKA MUSEET

30 PLACES
TO DISCOVER
WITH CHILDREN

The 5 best
PLAYGROUNDS

396 MULLE MECK-PARKEN
Mönstringsvägen 9
Solna ⑨
+46 (0)70 229 05 95

Mulle Meck, called Gary Gadget in English, is a Swedish children's book and computer game character with his own themed playground in Solna, made of scrap. In addition to all the characters from Mulle Meck's world, there is also a children's library with Bagar Birgit's pattisserie, which only open in summertime.

400 UGGLEPARKEN

397 RÅLAMBSHOVS- PARKEN PLAYGROUND

Smedsuddsvägen 6
Kungsholmen ⑧

This colourful, creative playground sparks children's imagination. Popular fairy-tale characters hang from the trees, and there are tiny puzzles and educational decoration everywhere. The carpentry workshop where children can build and create using pipes, planks and sticks is very popular.

398 ANDERS FRANZÉNS PARK

Båtklubbsgatan 2
Hammarby Sjöstad

It is not unusual for families to leave the frenetic city behind and visit Anders Franzéns Park in Hammarby Sjöstad. The playgrounds' design was inspired by the old shipyard that used to be here and is named after Anders Franzén, the amateur naval archaeologist who discovered the wreck of the Vasa galleon.

399 BRYGGARTÄPPAN

Bjurholmsgatan 1-A
Södermalm ⑤

An area hidden behind house façades and fences near Nytorget has been transformed into a miniature version of Södermalm, as featured in Per Anders Fogelström's classic novel *City of My Dreams*. Children can learn more about the old times, working with old tools in the smithy, or play hide-and-seek in the textile factory.

400 UGGLEPARKEN

AT: KRISTINEBERGS
SLOTTSPARK
Nordenflychts-
vägen 22-C
Kungsholmen ⑧

The locals call this playground Uggle-parken, because of its 5,5-metre-high owl-shaped slides. With mushrooms and beetles for children to climb, and a maze in the shape of an anthill, the Danish architects of Monstrum created a sustainable wooden playground that is both challenging and alluring for kids of all ages.

5 great
MUSEUMS FOR CHILDREN

401 SPÅRVÄGSMUSEET

Gasverkstorget 1
Norra Djurgårds-
staden ⑨
+46 (0)8 123 337 01
parvagsmuseet.se

Try driving a tram, dress up in a uniform, test whether you can run faster than a bus, or drive a mini underground train: at the Transport Museum, children can tons of fun. With its extensive collection of vintage vehicles and engaging displays, this museum provides a fascinating insight into the city's history of transportation.

402 NORDISKA MUSEET

Djurgårdsvägen 6-16
Djurgården ⑥
+46 (0)8 519 547 00
nordiskamuseet.se/en

This is a great place for anyone interested in a better understanding of the people of the Nordic region. A visit to the Children's Playhouse takes families back in time, to the 19th century. You will be surprised at how much kids enjoy 'milking cows' and weighing goods in the shop. Older kids, that are interested in time travel, should head to The Time Vault in the museum's cellar.

403 JUNIBACKEN

Galärvarvsvägen 8
Djurgården ⑥
+46 (0)8 587 230 00
junibacken.se

This cultural centre is all about Swedish children's literature, but especially about Astrid Lindgren. The amazing Story Train is the highlight of every visit but don't forget to see what's on in the temporary exhibition space, Pippi's house, the children's theatre and the bookshop, which is Sweden's biggest and a real treasure trove for young bookworms.

404 TOM TITS EXPERIMENT

Storgatan 33
Södertälje
+46 (0)8 550 225 00
tomtit.se

Tom Tits is just a 40-minute drive from Stockholm. In this former factory, kids can step into a world of scientific exploration and hands-on learning in technology, physics, maths, geography, biology and much more. This is a great day out for anyone who wants to have fun while expanding their knowledge and understanding of the world we live in.

405 POLISMUSEET

Museivägen 7
Gärdet ⑥
+46 (0)10 563 80 00
polismuseet.se

The Police Museum is an exciting destination for enthusiasts of sirens, blue lights, and mysteries. Children can dress up in police uniforms, operate radios, ride on police motorbikes, and do thrilling jobs in the police station. Tip: Outside the museum, there is also a fun police-themed playground which you can visit without having to pay admission.

5 places to go with
TEENAGERS

---

406 PARADOX MUSEUM

Sergelgatan 20
Norrmalm ①
+46 (0)8 91 16 61
*paradoxmuseum
stockholm.com*

With over 70 mind-bending optical illusions and paradoxes, this interactive museum will challenge your senses and expand your perception. Laugh, be amazed, and capture unforgettable moments with your mobile phone. To photograph the illusions in some of the rooms, the museum recommends that you are three in the room: one person to take the picture and two models.

407 FOTOGRAFISKA

Stadsgårds-
hamnen 22
Södermalm ⑤
+46 (0)8 509 005 00
fotografiska.com

In a world of visual content and social media, Fotografiska, Stockholm's museum of contemporary photography, offers a unique opportunity to broaden teenagers' perspectives. With captivating exhibitions and diverse narratives, the museum promotes dialogue and inspires artistic expression, fostering a broader appreciation for the power of visual storytelling and encouraging a deeper understanding of photography's impact on society.

408 SPACE & AVICII EXPERIENCE

Sergelgatan 2
Norrmalm ⓘ
space.cc
aviciiexperience.com

SPACE is a vibrant hub of youth culture. Being the world's largest permanent gaming centre, this place offers a safe and inclusive environment for tournaments, casual gaming, or simply having fun. Additionally, it features the immersive Avicii Experience exhibition, chronicling the life and music of the world famous and highly acclaimed Swedish DJ, musician, and producer Tim Bergling.

409 DOWNTOWN CAMPER BY SCANDIC

Brunkebergstorg 9
Norrmalm ⓘ
+46 (0)8 517 263 00
*scandichotels.com/
hotels/sweden*

Downtown Camper is a teen-friendly urban hotel with connecting rooms and shared social spaces for activities such as board games, ping pong, and shuffleboard. Their updated activity calendar includes parkour, yoga, and kayaking. Bicycles, longboards, and skateboards are available for rent in the lobby.

410 TEKNISKA MUSEET

Museivägen 7
Gärdet ⑥
+46 (0)8 450 56 00
tekniskamuseet.se

From robotics to space exploration and engineering marvels, the National Museum of Science and Technology offers a wide range of captivating activities that will spark children's interest in STEM subjects. While you're here, don't miss Wisdom - one of the world's most complex architectural structures. The very latest and most powerful 3D scientific visualisation technology has been installed inside the huge wooden spherical dome.

5 places where
BABIES CAN CRAWL AROUND FREELY

---

411 RUM FÖR BARN
AT: KULTURHUSET
Sergels torg
Norrmalm ①
+46 (0)8 506 202 73
*kulturhuset
stadsteatern.se*

Rum för Barn, on the fourth floor of Kulturhuset, is the perfect pitstop for families. This library is a peaceful place where children and adults can read books or enjoy story time together. Soft carpets, cosy reading corners, spacious toilets, and pleasant nursing rooms make this an all-time favourite escape in the city.

412 PLAYROOM BLUBB
AT: SJÖHISORISKA MUSEET
Djurgårdsbrunns-
vägen 24
Gärdet ⑥
+46 (0)8 519 549 00
www.sjohistoriska.se

After visiting the national maritime museum, immerse yourself in Blubb, a captivating underwater world for children. Kids can play and explore while their parents enjoy convenient amenities such as changing tables, a nursing room and a picnic area.

413 DIESELVERKSTADEN
Marcusplatsen 17
Sickla
+46 (0)8 718 82 90
dieselverkstaden.se

At Dieselverkstaden in Sickla, babies and toddlers can participate in baby rhythm and baby painting classes, the latter being especially popular. These activities, which are geared towards children aged 9-24 months, stimulate their senses, promote exploration, and provide a fun interactive experience for both babies and caregivers.

414 MELLANRUMMET

AT: STADSMUSEET
Ryssgården
Södermalm ⑤
+46 (0)8 508 316 20
stadsmuseet.stockholm

Stop in at the Stockholm City Museum for a toddler-friendly break. In Mellanrummet, the children's room, you can read, play, and heat a packed lunch. While some activities are geared towards older children, it also has space for toddlers to move around freely when they're done sitting in their pushchair.

415 FAMILY ARKDES

Exercisplan 4
Skeppsholmen ⑥
+46 (0)8 520 235 00
arkdes.se/family-arkdes

Who doesn't love an indoor playground that is also aesthetically pleasing for parents to spend time in? At ArkDes, the Swedish Centre for Architecture and Design, they have a welcoming and bright space with plush carpets, padded huts, and soft furnishings, as well as building blocks and books, encouraging children to explore.

415 FAMILY ARKDES

The 5 cutest
KIDS FASHION SHOPS

416 MINI RODINI

Odengatan 78
Vasastan ⑦
+46 (0)8 314 110
minirodini.com

Since its launch, Mini Rodini has attracted a lot of attention for its playful, humorous, aesthetic, and quirky designs with a 70's vibe. In fact, it's one of Scandinavia's fastest-growing kids' clothing brands. Visit the flagship store next to Vasaparken. You'll love all the animals, bright colours, and unisex prints.

417 BABYMOCS

Skånegatan 53
Södermalm ⑤
+46 (0)76 224 32 53
babymocs.com

BabyMocs Stockholm is a charming shop, selling a fashionable range of stylish and sustainable baby and children's products. Their speciality? Their moccasins, which are crafted from high-quality leather, providing comfort and flexibility for tiny feet. In addition to shoes, the shop also sells other clothing items and accessories, with a focus on quality, style, and eco-consciousness.

418 SEWING FOR SEEDS

Stora Nygatan 36
Gamla stan ③
sewingforseeds.se

Multi-brand store Sewing for Seeds is an exquisite, independent fashion boutique, selling beautifully crafted clothes and toys for babies and older children. Unlike most kid's shops, it has no social media presence or online store. The store's curated selection, including such brands as FUB and Swedish Silly Silas, makes it well worth visiting.

419 ECOSTHLM

Katarina Bangata 17
Södermalm ⑤
+46 (0)76 325 13 37
ecosthlm.se

EcoSTHLM is a leading destination for organic and non-toxic toys and children's products in the city. Founder Therese Blomqvist is committed to offering stylish and environmentally friendly items. Although the store largely focuses on toys, it also sells accessories such as hats, caps, socks, and beanies.

420 LILLA ETC

Odengatan 89
Vasastan ⑦
+46 (0)8 33 87 00
etcstores.se

Lilla ETC is a multi-brand store selling clothing and shoes for children from 0 to 10 years old, with cool prints, made of organic fabrics and in pretty colours. The place to go for mix and match items by brands such as Bobo Choses, MarMar and Joha. Don't forget to check out the irresistible, tiny Adidas tracksuits.

5 places to meet with
ANIMALS

---

421 STORA SKUGGANS 4H-GÅRD

Stora Skuggans
väg 40
Norra Djurgården ⑨
+46 (0)8 16 62 06
storaskuggans4hgard.se

The 4H global network pops up in several places across Stockholm. One of the most visited farms is Stora Skuggan, which was founded in 1984. They organise activities with their farm animals to help children develop into committed and responsible people with respect for the environment.

422 NYCKELVIKENS HERRGÅRD

Nyckelviksvägen 1
Nacka
+46 (0)8 718 00 21
*nyckelvikensherrgard.
se/bondgarden*

Nyckelviken is a firm favourite with many families. Children can visit the farm to see cows, horses, chickens, rabbits, sheep, and pigs graze in their pastures. The manor also has a cosy cafe. Additionally, there are spacious grassy areas for a family picnic. The unique landscape features ancient oak trees alongside preserved 18th-century buildings, creating a rich cultural environment.

423 ASPUDDSPARKEN

Hövdingagatan 15
Aspudden ④
+46 (0)8 19 99 15
aspuddsparken.se

Besides taking advantage of the playground and paddling pool, visitors of Aspuddsparken can also interact with and observe a variety of animals, including goats, pigs, sheep, rabbits, guinea pigs, cats, and horses. During spring and summer, there are lots of adorable baby animals. By mid-July, the horses, goats, and sheep temporarily move away to graze in the pastures over the summer.

424 LILL-SKANSEN

AT: SKANSEN
Djurgårds-
slätten 49-51
Djurgården ⑥
+46 (0)8 442 82 00
skansen.se

Since 1955, kids have been able to get up close and personal in the children's petting zoo at Skansen. Who doesn't love a cuddle with pet rabbits, pygmy goats and cute mini pigs? The oldest open-air museum in the world also has some species that are typical of Sweden, like bears, moose and wolves.

425 ELFVIKS GÅRD

Elfviks Uddväg 12
Lidingö
+46 (0)70 496 21 55
elfviksgard.nu

Nestled on the north-eastern part of Lidingö, this idyllic farm offers picturesque views of Stockholm's inlet and expansive meadows. Visitors can interact with a variety of animals, including horses, sheep, goats, rabbits, hens, and cats. Explore the charming farm shops that sell honey, candles, vintage items, and art, or indulge in a delightful lunch or *fika* at the bistro.

MISS CLARA

25 PLACES TO SLEEP

5 of the most
GLAMOROUS
hotels

---

426 HOTEL VILLA DAGMAR

Nybrogatan 25-27
Östermalm ②
+46 (0)8 122 135 50
hotelvilladagmar.com

Hotel Villa Dagmar, located on vibrant Nybrogatan, is synonymous with intimate elegance and luxury. Classic Swedish design blends seamlessly with modern sophistication in this meticulous restored historic villa. Culinary delights await at the acclaimed restaurant, and the hotel's wine bar Dagges is worth a visit in itself.

427 HOTEL KUNGSTRÄDGÅRDEN

Västra Trädgårds-
gatan 11-B
Norrmalm ①
+46 (0)8 440 66 50
hotelkungst
radgarden.se

The King's Garden is an independent family-owned hotel in an early-18th-century building. The rooms are a nice mix of classic Gustavian architecture with all the modern amenities you need. Sit down in the atrium and take in the scenery under the large glass roof.

428 BERNS HOTEL

Berzelii Park
Norrmalm ②
+46 (0)8 566 322 00
berns.se

Mythical Berns is a historic landmark that seamlessly combines old-world charm with contemporary luxury. The hotel offers a central location for easy exploration, exquisite rooms, a vibrant cultural scene, clubbing experiences, and delightful dining options.

429 HOTEL KUNG CARL

Birger Jarlsgatan 21
Norrmalm ①
+46 (0)8 463 50 00
kungcarl.se

Hotel Kung Carl in Stockholm is an artful blend of history and modernity. The boutique hotel has hosted Swedish luminaries such as Selma Lagerlöf, Greta Garbo and August Strindberg. Guests step into a world of elegance, spending the night in tastefully decorated rooms. If only the walls could talk!

430 NOBIS HOTEL

Norrmalmstorg 2-4
Norrmalm ②
+46 (0)8 614 10 00
nobishotel.se

A gold-framed bar, beautifully designed rooms and a fashionable address make this hotel just as elegant as it sounds. Claesson Koivisto Rune Architects designed the elegant, Scandi interior for this 19th-century building. The proximity to the city's glamorous shopping streets makes Nobis a great place to stay when visiting the capital.

427 HOTEL KUNGSTRÄDGÅRDEN

The 5 hippest
DESIGN HOTELS

---

431 MISS CLARA BY NOBIS

Sveavägen 48
Norrmalm ①
+46 (0)8 440 67 00
missclarahotel.com

This boutique hotel was named after Clara Strömberg, the head teacher of a girls' school in this building 100 years ago. Despite its long history, the hotel has a young, stylish vibe and the architect, Gert Wingårdh, delicately blended the original art nouveau details with timeless materials and modern design icons.

432 BLIQUE BY NOBIS

Gävlegatan 18
Vasastan ⑦
+46 (0)8 557 666 00
bliquebynobis.se

At Blique, design takes centre stage. Architect Gert Wingårdh has transformed this iconic former warehouse into a modern hotel, with its harmonious fusion of old-world industrial grandeur and innovative Scandinavian minimalism. The Blique has become one of Stockholm's creative hubs, with its art collabs, multiple restaurants and generous spaces.

433 HOTEL SKEPPSHOLMEN

Gröna gången 1
Skeppsholmen ⑥
+46 (0)8 407 23 00
hotelskeppsholmen.se

Hotel Skeppsholmen is a lovely, tranquil oasis in the heart of the city. It was originally built in the late 1600s but has since been transformed into a modern hotel, blending historic charm with stylish sophistication in a serene retreat.

434 **AT SIX**

Brunkebergstorg 6
Norrmalm ⓘ
+46 (0)8 578 828 00
hotelatsix.com

Contemporary art, design, and architecture – does this sound like an intriguing combination? The luxurious At Six hotel boasts spacious rooms, top-notch amenities and a sophisticated atmosphere. London-based Universal Design Studio signed off on the elegant decoration scheme, filling the rooms with original artwork.

435 **HOBO**

Brunkebergstorg 4
Norrmalm ⓘ
+46 (0)8 578 827 00
hobo.se

Newly renovated Brunkeberg Square in the city centre has become a place where people like to meet up. The convivial atmosphere has been enhanced by the Hobo Hotel with its hip, urban design by Berlin-based architect Werner Aisslinger. Its impeccable service and laidback ambience make this a popular place, where guests can enjoy a vibrant blend of modern comfort and artistic expression

434 AT SIX

5

AFFORDABLE

places to sleep

---

436 GENERATOR HOSTELS

Torsgatan 10
Norrmalm ①
+46 (0)8 505 323 70
*staygenerator.com/
hostels/stockholm*

Travellers who prefer to blow their budget on anything but accommodation (but who still appreciate cool design) should check out Generator's first branch in Stockholm. Centrally located at Torsgatan, and a brisk walk from the city's Central Station, this trendy hostel offers both dorms and private rooms.

437 BO HOTEL

Arenavägen 69
Johanneshov
+46 (0)8 121 357 30
bohotel.se

Bo Hotel is a short metro ride to the south of the city, next to Globen (Avicii Arena). Every type of traveller can find suitable accommodation here. Families will love the colourful superior rooms with comfortable king size beds, while flexible short term-visitors might prefer the compact sleeping units.

438 REIMERSHOLME HOTEL

Reimersholms-
gatan 5
Reimersholme ④
+46 (0)8 444 48 88
reimersholmehotel.se

Discover this hotel at Reimersholme, on the island of the same name. After a walk or a short bus ride from Hornstull, you end up at this budget-friendly hotel, which has much more to offer than just accommodation. Enjoy intimate concerts and live events at their bar and restaurant. Don't forget to check out Stockholm's most secret natural wine bar upstairs.

439 HOTEL WITH URBAN DELI

Sveavägen 44
Norrmalm ①
+46 (0)8 30 30 50
hotelwith.se

If you prefer a quiet night, visit Hotel With. None of the underground rooms have windows, but the modern interior and state-of-the-art technology largely make up for this. The hotel belongs to Urban Deli, the popular restaurant, bar and supermarket upstairs, where you can enjoy some of the best views in the city from the roof terrace.

440 ZZZ DREAMSCAPE HOTEL

Kungsgatan 17
Norrmalm ①
+46 (0)8 507 331 00
zzzdreamscapehotel.se

Hotel Zzz in Stockholm is just the place to go if you're looking for somewhere comfortable and budget-friendly to stay. With its central location, simple but relaxing underground rooms, and digital solutions instead of staff, this no-frills option caters to travellers who are looking for somewhere affordable without compromising on basic amenities. A great option for an easy and hassle-free stay in Stockholm.

5
UNUSUAL
places to sleep

441 BANK HOTEL

Arsenalsgatan 6
Norrmalm ②
+46 (0)8 598 580 00
bankhotel.se

This boutique hotel is located on one of Stockholm's most prestigious backstreets that leads from glittering Nybroviken to Kungsträdgården. As its name indicates, the building is a former bank, as you can tell by the imposing bronze entrance doors, the glamorous bank vault and the 'smash the piggy bank' dessert on the restaurant's menu.

442 BACKSTAGE HOTEL

Djurgårdsvägen 68
Djurgården ⑥
+46 (0)8 502 541 40
backstagehotel
sthlm.com

The atmosphere in this hotel is akin to being 'backstage' – a place where artists and performers prepare, connect, and unwind. With its stylish design, vibrant ambience, and proximity to the ABBA Museum, Cirkus and Hasselbacken's live performances in their garden, the Backstage Hotel is your gateway to a world of enticing cultural events.

443 LÅNGHOLMEN HOTEL

Långholmsmuren 20
Södermalm ④
+46 (0)8 720 85 00
langholmen.com

Ever fancied spending the night in prison? Probably not, but Långholmen Hotel offers just that: a really captivating experience. From the 18th century until 1974, Långholmen was the city's prison island. Today it is a popular, verdant oasis. Sleep in stylish cells and grab a bite in the welcoming Finkan pub.

444 SVARTSÖ LOGI

Jetty: Alsviks brygga
Ahlsvik
Svartsö
svartsologi.se

Svartsö Logi in the archipelago is the perfect place for anyone who enjoys the luxuries of hotel accommodation and the escapism and adventure of sleeping in nature. In summertime they have five furnished canvas tents with small terraces, lounge chairs and lake views. Book well ahead – this is glamping at its best!

445 THE WINERY HOTEL

Rosenborgsgatan 20
Solna
+46 (0)8 14 60 00
thewineryhotel.se

The Winery is Sweden's first boutique and urban winery hotel. The huge brick building is just a short drive, out of town. Here you will find in-house wine production and industrial chic hotel rooms with a warm ambience. The rooftop terrace is the perfect place to escape with an outstanding glass of wine in hand.

5 intimate
BOUTIQUE HOTELS

---

446 ETT HEM

Sköldungagatan 2
Östermalm ①
+46 (0)8 20 05 90
etthem.se

Ett Hem has managed to establish a reputation for itself as Stockholm's most luxurious and intimate hotel. With just a few rooms and suites designed by the British designer Ilse Crawford, this exclusive 'inner sanctum' offers a personal and discrete service. Once you've checked in here, you'll never want to leave.

447 THE SPARROW HOTEL

Birger Jarlsgatan 24
Norrmalm ②
+46 (0)8 122 173 00
www.thesparrow.se

This French-inspired accommodation next to Stureplan stands out because of its consummate attention to detail. The hotel boasts tastefully decorated rooms, where guests can tuck into a delectable breakfast buffet with freshly baked baguettes and croissants. Even if you don't stay at the hotel, do check out their French wine bar and bistro, which are definitely worth visiting.

448 HOTEL FRANTZ

Peter Myndes
backe 5
Södermalm ⑤
+46 (0)8 442 16 80
hotelfrantz.se

If you want to be close to all that Södermalm has to offer, Hotel Frantz at Slussen ticks all the boxes. This trendy, small, family-owned accommodation features individually decorated rooms with modern amenities and a unique, cosy ambiance.

449 LYDMAR HOTEL

Södra Blasieholms-
hamnen 2
Norrmalm ②
+46 (0)8 22 31 60
lydmar.com

The Lydmar, a boutique hotel that embodies a refined sense of luxury and sophistication, has a prime waterfront location opposite Stockholm Palace. The hotel is renowned for its art exhibitions, live music, relaxed atmosphere, and homey feeling. Tip: enjoy the amazing views from the patio or terrace.

450 HOTEL RUTH

Surbrunnsgatan 38
Vasastan ⑦
+46 (0)8 15 04 20
hotelruth.se

Hotel Ruth, which is one block away from buzzing Odengatan, is a tranquil haven for both visitors and residents. This boutique gem in a classic Stockholm building captures the essence of Vasastan with a harmonious blend of global influences and local charm. Indulge in their signature breakfast, which includes a most delightful combination of cream cake and bubbly.

CENTRALBADET

25 WEEKEND ACTIVITIES

———

5 of the best places to
SWIM

---

451 CENTRALBADET

Drottninggatan 88
Norrmalm ①
+46 (0)8 545 213 00
centralbadet.se

Escape the hustle and bustle in Drottninggatan and slip into a lush oasis. Centralbadet is located in a beautiful and well-preserved art nouveau palace that was built in 1909. Here you can try different types of therapeutic baths along with spa treatments and swim in the pool which has been here since 1904.

452 LÅNGHOLMEN ISLAND

Södermalm ④

The idyllic island of Långholmen near Södermalm, with a view over Riddarfjärden, is a popular spot for picnics and swimming in summertime. On hot days, the beach can get quite crowded, but it's great for families with kids. If you prefer to dive off cliffs you will find that there too, as well as a jetty.

453 STUREBADET

Sturegallerian 36
Östermalm ②
+46 (0)8 545 015 00
sturebadet.se

Step back in time in this gorgeous spa, which dates from 1885. Sturebadet was built in the art nouveau style by the architect Hjalmar Molin. The 29-degree swimming pool, saunas, gym equipment and spa treatments make this the perfect getaway to treat your body and mind.

454 HORNSBERGS STRANDPARK

Hornbergs strand 41
Stadshagen
Kungsholmen Ⓑ

The former industrial area in northwestern Kungsholmen has been transformed into the flourishing Hornsberg neighbourhood. There are three long floating piers along the waterfront facing Ulvsundasjön, which are perfect for outdoor swimming and which are very popular with the locals and joggers. The park also has a shower, with solar power heating up the water.

455 FORSGRÉNSKA BADET

Medborgarplatsen 6
Södermalm Ⓢ
+46 (0)8 508 403 20
motionera.stockholm/
forsgrenska-badet

This indoor swimming pool in Södermalm is a popular place, with its 25-metre pool and stunning windows. Fun facts: During the renovation of Medborgarhuset, where the baths are located, workers discovered a time capsule from 1938, containing historic artefacts. A new time capsule was created for the reopening, with old and new items relating to the building.

The 5 best places for
OUTDOOR RUNNING

---

456 NORRA DJURGÅRDEN
Norra Djurgården ⑨

You can enter the green area of Norra Djurgården from different directions. Either you start at Stadion and jog through Lill-Janskogen, or you start from Ropsten, Hjorthagen or Universitetet. Regardless, you will run through lush woodland, past towering oak trees, up and down steep hills.

457 TANTOLUNDEN
Zinkens Väg
Södermalm ⑤

One of the city's largest parks is located in the southeastern part of Södermalm. Tantolunden was established around the turn of the last century and developed into a popular meeting spot for people of all ages. Combine jogging with exercises in the wooden outdoor gym and finish your work-out with a dip in Lake Årstaviken.

458 HAGAPARKEN
Solna ⑨

This is Stockholm's very own Hyde Park. Inspired by English landscape gardens, the park is also home to several royal buildings and the special Copper Tents. Enjoy the nature and the historical architecture while running around Haga or take the long run lap around nearby Brunnsviken.

459 RÅLAMBSHOVS-PARKEN

Smedsuddsvägen /
Rålambshovsleden
Kungsholmen ⑧

The running trail around Riddarfjärden is unbeatable. Covering a distance of roughly 7 kilometres, it winds its way past the Old Town, Söder Mälarstrand, Västerbron and Kungsholmen, offering views of the glittering water wherever you are. Rålambshovsparken is a good place to start as it has an outdoor gym where you can warm up.

460 DJURGÅRDEN ISLAND

Djurgården ⑥

Djurgården used to be the King's hunting grounds. Situated across the water, within view of the Royal Palace, this lush island is a firm favourite with Stockholmers. Besides museums and cafes, you'll also find a 10-kilometre running trail along the shoreline, with oak trees and pretty meadows.

458 HAGAPARKEN

The 5 best
BIKE RIDES

---

461 ULRIKSDAL TO DJURGÅRDEN

The fastest way to explore both Northern *(norra)* and Southern *(södra)* Djurgården (the latter is the island mostly referred to as just 'Djurgården') is probably by bike. Start from Ulriksdal Palace and bike south towards the northeastern shoreline of Lake Brunnsviken. Take a left before the Swedish Museum of Natural History and continue towards Stockholm Royal Seaport. Cross Gärdet before you reach Djurgårdsbrunn after 12 kilometres.

462 STOCKHOLM TO NYNÄSHAMN

Choose the Nynäsleden trail if you prefer a more challenging distance. Drive south until you reach Länna, then continue through beautiful Södertörn until you reach Nynäshamn. This 90-km trail is well-known for the variety it offers, with plenty of nature, old runes, fine lakes where you can bathe, and historical landscapes.

463 AROUND LIDINGÖ

Lidingö Island in the inner Stockholm archipelago is known for its Cross-Country Race, which is the largest around the world with approximately 60.000 participants every year. If you do not want to tackle the 30 kilometres on foot, hop on a bike instead. Offers plenty of stunning scenery and hilly terrain.

464 CITY CENTRE TO DROTTNINGHOLM

The islands in Lake Mälaren have a stunning landscape, with old churches, magnificent castles, farm shops and plenty of lush nature. Leaving the city centre, you reach Drottningholm Palace after about 13 kilometres if you ride through Kungsholmen. From there you can either continue to Ekerö or wind your way around Lovön before turning back.

465 HELLASGÅRDEN

The cycle trails around Hellasgården in Nackareservatet to the south-east of Stockholm City are very popular with mountain bikers. The nature reserve has pine trees, small lakes and rocky outcrops. There are several trails here but two of the most popular routes are the 10-kilometre-long Blå Spåret and Gröna Spåret.

5

ADVENTUROUS ACTIVITIES *to try*

---

466 **KAJAKKOMPANIET**
   Kristinebergs strand
   Kungsholmen ⑧
   +46 (0)8 22 48 18
   kajakkompaniet.se

Explore Stockholm from the water in a single or double kayak. Kajakkompaniet offers trips around Kungsholmen or Långholmen but you can also paddle yourself if you don't like guided tours. Cruising around the capital on long, cloudless summer evenings can be an extraordinary experience.

470 **RIB-BOAT**

467 LUFTBALLONG

Koltrastvägen 21
Sollentuna
+46 (0)8 92 02 02
ballong.se

Take high altitude to a new level during a trip in a hot air balloon. As this activity is very dependent on the weather, this will only go ahead on cloudless evenings. Watch the sky turn pink and see how Stockholm's islands are connected.

468 KLÄTTERVERKET

Gasverksvägen 15
Norra Djurgården ⑨
+46 (0)8 641 10 48
klatterverket.se

Combine some physical activity with an exploration of Stockholm's history. Klätterverket is housed inside one of the old gas metering buildings of the adjacent gasworks. This is a cultural monument and as you climb you can still see traces of industrial history including pipes and wires.

469 SUP

AT: SURFBUSSEN
Kungsholms
strand 181
Kungsholmen ⑧
+46 (0)8 21 33 33
surfbussen.nu

All the way from Hawaii, SUP surfing (Stand-Up-Paddling) has finally made it to Karlbergssjön in Stockholm. This offshoot of surfing has you standing on your board using a paddle to propel yourself through the water. Karlbergskanalen is a nice canal with calm water where you can paddle towards City Hall. A great work-out for your core, shoulders and balance.

470 RIB-BOAT

AT: ÖPPET HAV
Sjövillan 208
Skeppsholmen ⑥
+46 (0)8 500 332 21
oppethav.se

Whizz through the archipelago in RIB-boats (rigid-hulled inflatable boats) at a top speed of 60 knots. This is an amazing experience on days when the water shimmers like a mirror but thanks to the manoeuvrability and the power of the engines, you still feel as if you are 'skimming the surface' in less conditions.

5 interesting
DAY TRIPS

471 MARIEFRED
visitsormland.com

Mariefred is next to Lake Mälaren, about 50 kilometres west of Stockholm. The small town is built around Gripsholm Castle from 1537. You can also find a museum of graphic design and various restaurants, shops and cafes here. Tip: during summertime take the 100-year-old Mariefred steamship from Stockholm.

472 VÄRMDÖ
visitvarmdo.com

The vast island of Värmdö is located in the innermost part of the archipelago. Go by car to check out various destinations. Besides must-sees like Artipelag, Värmdö Musteri and Gustavberg's porcelain factory, visit the sea baths or have a drink in one of the charming cafes.

473 SIGTUNA
destinationsigtuna.se

Sweden's oldest town is located less than an hour from Stockholm. Sigtuna was founded in 980 AD and is known for its fascinating history with rune stones and old church ruins as well as for its picturesque, pedestrian-friendly town centre with cafes, restaurants and small shops in charming wooden houses.

474 **UPPSALA**

destinationuppsala.se

Even though Uppsala is one of Sweden's largest cities, it has retained a sense of small-town charm and personality. This university town offers historically interesting attractions, a lush countryside and the liveliness of a big city. Uppsala is a convenient day trip destination. You can easily get there by train in 40 minutes from Stockholm.

475 **SANDHAMN**

destination sandhamn.se

This island in the outer Stockholm archipelago has been popular for pleasure boating since the late 19th century. Sandhamn is worth a visit all year round and a perfect destination in summertime for a day at the beach, a seafood lunch in the sun, or a stroll down the charming gravel alleys or along the harbour.

472 **ARTIPELAG AT VÄRMDÖ**

GAMLA STAN

25 RANDOM FACTS & GOOD-TO-KNOWS

5 fascinating
B O O K S
about Stockholm

---

476 CITY OF MY DREAMS
BY PER ANDERS
FOGELSTRÖM
1960

The *City Novels* by Swedish author Per Anders Fogelström are probably the most classic portrayal of Stockholm. The series describes the lives of successive generations of Stockholmers between 1860 and 1968 and in the first book, *City of My Dreams*, the narrative follows a group of working-class people on Södermalm during the late 1800s.

477 SWEDISH TRADITIONS
BY JAN-ÖJVIND SWAHN
2012

Whether you are interested in the classic Swedish traditions or prefer to discover the new, urban Stockholm, it may be fun to understand the background behind Swedish culture. In this book, the author and researcher Jan-Öjvind Swahn explains everything from the frog dance in Midsummer to the Lucia festival in December.

478 DOKUMENT STOCKHOLM
BY JEPPE WIKSTRÖM
2008

This is the largest photographic documentation project about Stockholm in modern times. With over 1000 images, some photos even date from the early 1850s. This fascinating thick book offers a unique picture of the Swedish capital and how it developed through the decades.

479 TRION
BY JOHANNA HEDMAN
2021

Johanna Hedman's debut novel *Trion* is a bittersweet story about three young people in Stockholm. They are in their twenties, a time in life when everything seems possible and impossible at the same time. The main characters move between places such as Lärkstan, Mariatorget, Rönnells and cafe Ritorno, the Royal Library, and the university.

480 SWEDEN: A CRIME FICTION WONDERLAND
BY ANITA SHENOI
2016

Understand why the most beautiful places in Sweden and Stockholm have become the setting for some of the most intriguing crime writing in modern time. This book is for those of you who can just not get enough of the Nordic Noir genre's tension between the tranquil social surface in Scandinavia and the horror beneath.

5
FILMS
set in Stockholm

---

481 **THE SQUARE**
2017

Ruben Östlund's satirical drama about a curator of a contemporary art museum in Stockholm is an unusual work with challenging themes that won a Golden Palm in Cannes. Odenplan, Central Station and The Royal Palace's outer courtyard play a key role in this acclaimed film.

482 **KÄRLEK & ANARKI**
2020

Kärlek & Anarki is a comedy-drama series by Lisa Langseth. It follows the lives of Sofie, a married consultant, and Max, a young IT technician, as they engage in an unexpected flirt at the publishing house where they work. The series showcases iconic Stockholm locations such as Sergels torg, Lärkstan, and Kungsträdgården.

483 **STOCKHOLM STORIES**
2014

Directed by Karin Fahlén, *Stockholm Stories* is a multi-plot drama about five people whose paths cross during a few rainy days in November. In this contemporary comedy, the characters visit several places that you'll recognise, from Gondolen, Hötorgsskraporna and Millesgården to the Parliament House.

484 **SUMMER WITH MONIKA**
1953

Experience the Swedish summer in the archipelago in black and white in this Ingmar Bergman film from 1953. Two working-class teenagers start a passionate love affair and steal a boat to be with one another during an idyllic summer. Things do not turn out as planned when autumn arrives.

485 **WE ARE THE BEST!**
2013

Lukas Moodysson's drama from 2013 is a lovely nostalgic trip back to the eighties. In a heartfelt and hilarious story about the teenage years, this film follows three rebellious girls in 1982 Stockholm who decide to form a punk band, despite being told by everyone that punk is dead.

5

IMPORTANT DATES

in Stockholm's history

486 **1252**

The oldest preserved written document referring to Stockholm is a letter written by the statesman Birger Jarl to King Valdemar from 1252. No one knows for sure where the city's name originated but one theory is that the words *stock* (log) and *holm* (little island) refer to the city's distinctive bridges and waterways.

487 **8-10 NOVEMBER 1520**

In the 16th century, Danish forces invaded Sweden under the command of King Christian II. The series of events that took place in November 1520 was named the Stockholm Bloodbath since just under 100 aristocrats were executed at Stortorget in the Old Town. The event earned the king the nickname of Christian Tyrant.

488 6 JUNE 1523

Every year on Swedish National Day, people ask themselves: what are we actually celebrating? Remarkably enough, only a few Swedes know that this day marks the day in 1523 when Gustav Vasa besieged and captured Stockholm, after which he became the king. This ended the Kalmar Union and Sweden became a free kingdom.

489 16 MARCH 1792

Under the reign of Gustav III (1771-1792), Stockholm developed culturally. But the king was not that popular, especially with the nobility. At midnight on 16 March 1792, Gustav III was shot during a masked ball at the Royal Opera House, and died a few weeks later.

490 16 MAY 1930

The third Stockholm Exhibition, which was inaugurated on 16 May 1930, is a significant event in the history of architecture in Stockholm as it established Functionalism as the dominant architectural style in Sweden. The fair's ideas about stripped-down, bright and functional homes still live on, influencing Swedish housing to this day.

5

GOOD-TO-KNOW THINGS

---

491 LOCAL MONEY

Sweden is leading the race to becoming a cashless society. Many of the parking metres require you to download an app if you want to use them. Shops, cafes and even tourist attractions only accept bank cards or mobile phone payments, and Swish has become Sweden's go-to payment app.

492 DO'S

Here are some things that set Stockholm apart from other cities: you can drink the super fresh tap water, the capital is one of the most connected cities in Europe with access to free Wi-Fi in many places and adults travelling with strollers don't have to pay on public buses.

493 DON'T'S

Bear in mind that many smaller restaurants close in July. Also, tipping is not compulsory. Swedes love order so never jump a queue. You'll meet with angry stares if you do. And always look for the queueing ticket machines before joining a queue.

494 **GETTING AROUND**

Walking is a perfect way to explore Stockholm but if you prefer to give your feet a rest public transportation is an efficient way to get around. Tickets can be purchased in metro stations or from agents (such as Pressbyrån or 7-Eleven) or using the SL app. You cannot buy tickets on board of the bus.

495 **LANGUAGE**

Thanks to the education system and because Swedes in general take a keen cultural interest in English-spoken media, they speak excellent English for the most part. Despite this, Swedes can be a bit reticent when it comes to demonstrating their skills but they are also very nice and helpful.

5 essential
WEBSITES & APPS

───────

496 **THE LOCAL**
thelocal.se

The Local was founded in 2004 when two Brits moved to Stockholm. Offering an entertaining mix of daily news, current events, business and features, this English-language digital news publisher makes Swedish affairs accessible to an international audience. An easy way to keep up with all the latest news.

497 **VISIT STOCKHOLM**
visitstockholm.com

Owned by the City of Stockholm, Visit Stockholm is the official guide to the capital. Their website gives you updated tips about everything from where to find Wi-Fi to an extensive event calendar. Stop by their visitor centre in Kulturhuset at Sergels torg for personal assistance with questions concerning your stay in Stockholm.

498 SL TRAVEL PLANNER
sl.se

The easiest way to plan your journey in Stockholm by metro, rail, tram and bus is to use the travel planning tools on SL's homepage or app. Choose between real time departures if you are on the go, or scheduled departures if you want to plan ahead – both tools are available in English.

499 ARTWORKS
artworks.io

As already mentioned in the chapter on culture, Stockholm has a wide range of museums and art galleries – but navigating them can be a bit tricky at times. Artworks matches your location with local art venues and street art, providing information about current, past and upcoming shows in addition to helping you purchase unique pieces.

500 BRICK
brick.tech

Is your battery running low after a day of Stockholm's parks and museums? Brick has a network of charging stations in the city centre. Simply rent a power bank through their app for a fee so you can charge your phone on the go. Use the app's map function to locate the nearest charging station.

INDEX

COLOPHON

EDITING *and* COMPOSING — Antonia af Petersens

GRAPHIC DESIGN — Joke Gossé and doublebill.design

PHOTOGRAPHY — Nadja Endler — www.nadjaendler.se

p. 20-21: Magnus Skoglöf — p. 24: Fredrik Skogkvist, Magnus Skoglöf — p. 64: Idha Lindhag —
p. 85: Hanna Wolff — p. 91: Joakim Hovrevik — p. 180 (below): Artipelag — p. 236: Öppet Hav —
p. 239: Artipelag

COVER IMAGE — Kina Slott (secret 276)

D/2023/12.005/11

ISBN 978 94 6058 3452

NUR 510, 512

© 2018 Luster, Antwerp
Third edition, July 2023 — Second reprint, July 2023
lusterpublishing.com — THE500HIDDENSECRETS.COM
info@lusterpublishing.com

Printed in Italy by Printer Trento.

MIX
Paper | Supporting
responsible forestry
FSC® C015829